Ernesto Cardenal

MARILYN MONROE
AND OTHER POEMS

*Also by Ernesto Cardenal
and published by Search Press*

LOVE
IN CUBA

Ernesto Cardenal

MARILYN MONROE
AND OTHER POEMS

Oración por Marilyn Monroe
y otros poemas

Translated from the Spanish
by Robert Pring-Mill

Search Press London

First published in this translation
in Great Britain in 1975
by Search Press Limited
2–10 Jerdan Place London SW6 5PT

Published originally by
Ediciones Carlos Lohle, Buenos Aires, Ediciones
Ecuador, Mexico City, and others
in *Antologia, Homenaje a los Indios Americanos* and
other collections

Spanish originals © Ernesto Cardenal 1947, 1960, 1966, 1969, 1970, 1973, 1974
These translations © Ernesto Cardenal & Robert Pring-Mill 1974, 1975
Introduction © Robert Pring-Mill 1975

ALL RIGHTS RESERVED NO PART OF THIS PUBLICATION MAY BE STORED IN A RETRIEVAL SYSTEM TRANSMITTED OR REPRODUCED IN ANY FORM OR BY ANY MEANS KNOWN OR AS YET UNKNOWN WHETHER MANUSCRIPT ELECTRONIC MECHANICAL CHEMICAL PHOTOCOPYING RECORDING OR OTHERWISE FOR ANY PURPOSE WHATSOEVER IN ANY COUNTRY WITHOUT THE PREVIOUS WRITTEN PERMISSION OF SEARCH PRESS 2–10 JERDAN PLACE LONDON SW6 5PT GREAT BRITAIN

ALL APPLICATIONS FOR READING BROADCASTING PERFORMING ANTHOLOGY AND OTHER RIGHTS MUST BE ADDRESSED TO SEARCH PRESS

Printed and bound in Great Britain
by The Bowering Press, Limited, Plymouth
ISBN 0 85532 358 2

Contents

Introduction	7
Omagua	33
Above the rain-soaked track	35
Childhood in León	36
Watch how you behave	38
Costa-Rican roses	39
Imitation of Propertius	40
For twenty years	41
You?	42
That street with yellow lights	43
Shots last night	44
Carters sing	45
Epitaph for Adolfo Báez Bone	46
Somoza unveils his statue	47
Our poems cannot be published	48
Have you not read, my love?	49
Heavy raindrops	50
You came in dreams	51
Nearest me	52
Zero hour	53
NNW	54
A hum of tractors	56
Jet at evening	57
In the woods	58
The marmots are not dead	59
Behind the monastery	60

Lost cities	61
Vale of Cuernavaca	64
On Lake Nicaragua	67
Destruction of Santiago de Quauhtemalan	68
Managua 6.30 pm	73
Unrighteous Mammon	74
Prayer for Marilyn Monroe	75
Blessed is the man (Ps. 1)	78
Why hast thou forsaken me? (Ps. 22)	79
Thou art our ally Lord (Ps. 35)	81
Their shares shall wither as the grass (Ps. 37)	83
Hear this all you peoples (Ps. 49)	85
Apocalypse	87
Quetzal feathers dry—in time	93
Economy of Tahuantinsuyu	97
Katun 11 Ahau	105
Night	108
Tahirassawichi in Washington	113
In the half-light	117
Death of Thomas Merton	119
Glossary	135

Introduction

Ernesto Cardenal was born in 1925, in a sleepy tropical town called Granada. Its population of forty thousand makes it the third city of Nicaragua. In feeling, it is not unlike its Andalusian namesake, although it stands close to a volcano and on the shores of an extensive inland sea. The Gran Lago de Nicaragua is the largest landlocked body of water between the Great Lakes and Lake Titicaca, ninety-two miles long and thirty-four miles wide. It is little more than a hundred feet above sea-level, but twin volcanoes rise out of the lake itself about five thousand feet.

At its southern end, near the Costa-Rican border, there is a group of over thirty jungled islands—the Solentiname Archipelago. These, like Santorini, are the remnants of what was formerly another great volcanic cone. The largest of the islands, about three miles in length, is Mancarrón. It has a low bulging promontory jutting out north-west towards the distant capital, Managua, which has twice been destroyed by earthquakes since Ernesto Cardenal was born. On this lonely promontory, Cardenal, who had been ordained not long before, started clearing the jungle early in 1966, and founded a small Catholic community called Our Lady of Solentiname.

Cardenal is the only priest there, and the community is small and informal—much more of a "commune" than a community. Besides Cardenal, there are just three Nicaraguan lads from *campesino*—or peasant—families, a young married couple from Colombia with two small children, and the occasional visitor like myself. There is scant ritual and no written constitution

("The first rule is that there are no formal rules", Cardenal says), but I felt the presence of a deep spirituality. There is a good deal of meditation and a great amount of hard work—agriculture, fishing, handicrafts (Cardenal has built up a flourishing group of "primitive" painters in the commune and among the islanders). The living conditions are roughly those of the *campesinos*, though water has been piped up from the lake, and there is a small electric generator supplying light for private study.

The commune eats what the island and the lake provide. Fish is there in abundance for the catching. Meat is less frequent: chicken, iguana, or an armadillo, and sometimes wild pig or a deer when someone on the island has been hunting. But the staple foods are the *campesino*'s typical rice and beans (called *gallo pinto* when served together), maize, yucca, breadfruit, papayas, mangoes, avocados, plaintains, and sweet bananas of a number of kinds. Most of these grow within a hundred yards of the thatched huts.

To get there from civilization, as we know it, is a laborious task, but on most days a few islanders drop in, perhaps for medicine, advice, or just a chat. On Sundays, they come from surrounding islands in small boats—sometimes rowing two hours each way, and often in torrential rain—to share in an informal dialogue mass in the cool church, which stands on the neck of land between two jungled inlets. Cardenal encourages a full and free discussion of the bible readings, which tends to dwell particularly on their social relevance.

On a clear day, three graceful volcanoes cap the skyline to the south, in Costa Rica, but during the rainy season there are few clear skies, and I usually saw no further through the clammy haze than the mangrove swamps which line the mainland, about four miles away. Snakes, tarantulas and scorpions are all quite common, and enormous toads stared up at my torch on the paths at night. Periodically, an army of warrior-ants—*las guerreadoras* —came through the site, working its way methodically through each hut in turn (one simply moves out while they are present).

After rain, butterflies by the dozen competed with humming-birds to sip at enormous red-and-yellow flowers. In the early morning, *congo* monkeys screeched in the high trees across the nearest bay, and birds honked or hooted or screamed. There are many kinds of birds: herons like sentinels at the water's edge, each fishing its own territory, duck further out in the two bays, parrots, parrokeets, macaws ... All this, however, is the exotic surface of the place.

Such details do little to convey the inner beauty of Solentiname: its loneliness and peace, and spiritual simplicity. Even allowing for those inward features, one would scarcely expect such a remote and tiny commune to have any effect on the world from which it seems to have withdrawn, but the figure at its heart is more than the leader of what might have been just another "drop-out" group. Ernesto Cardenal has a powerful, but in many ways a naive, mind: he sees things more simply than most people do, takes intellectual short-cuts through quite thorny thickets, goes to the Christian "heart of the matter" in most dilemmas—whereas the structure of the world in which we live imposes devious ways, in which to miss the point, on most of us. Though by nature a rather silent man, he does not keep silent in the kinds of situation which tend to make us keep our own opinions to ourselves.

He has a double vocation, as a revolutionary Catholic priest and as a socially committed poet. In both these capacities, he can command attention not merely outside Solentiname itself but well beyond his native Nicaragua, appealing to the idealism of a whole generation throughout Latin America, and speaking with a Third World voice to all of us in Europe. Nor is his "message" an exclusively Christian one—though he deems it wholly meaningful only when viewed within a Christian frame-work—but rather one which makes a measure of good sense to all who are distressed by social injustice. He regards his two vocations as interlocking in a rather special way, seeing the figure of the "poet-priest" as having perhaps a better claim to being one of "the unacknowledged legislators of the world" than the ordinary run of socially committed poets.

Socially relevant poetry is a well-established genre in Latin America. Most modern Latin American creative writing has a political dimension and displays some kind of social concern. This gives writers a sense of mission: something of a conscious awareness that it is their "moral duty" to act as the guide and conscience of their people. Within this general context, poetry (briefer, more memorable, more readily diffused) has a special function. Much twentieth-century verse is specifically "protest poetry": poetry not merely aware of its society, but reacting against its patent errors and defects. In a continent where social and political injustice is so obvious, that is not at all surprising.

Such poetry is unlike most of that with which most of us are familiar. It is also read by people who bring different expectations to the act of reading. Over here, some might tend to look down on anyone who used the art of poetry to preach a "message" (any message), but in Latin America the committed poets and their public regard a poetic cult of art for art's sake as escapism—an evasion of the moral duty any writer's social conscience should impose on him. Protest poetry is seen as having a functional role in the process of social change.

The poet, writing from the standpoint of some specific ideology, wishes to promote what he sees as the proper sense of values in as many people as he can. This need to communicate to a wide audience imposes clarity of expression on the way in which he writes. Over here, we are perhaps too ready to assume that poems which are both clear and in some sense didactic are bound to be unsubtle. The poetry of Ernesto Cardenal shows this is not always true.

The founder of modern Spanish American poetry was a Nicaraguan: Rubén Darío (1867–1916), the father of *modernismo*. Darío's primarily Symbolist heritage still bears down on his fellow countrymen. To some extent, Cardenal's success in establishing his individual style is measured by the progress of his gradual escape from *modernista* pressures. Here "commitment" has helped: Darío was an art-for-art's-sake man, and could scarcely be described as a "committed poet" except, perhaps, in the more patriotic parts of *Cantos de vida y esperanza* (Songs of Life and Hope) (1905).

In Latin America, committed poetry began in earnest with Pablo Neruda (1904–73), the Chilean winner of the 1971 Nobel Prize for Literature, who stopped writing purely personal verse during the Spanish Civil War. He taught a generation of younger poets a new rhetoric of praise and dispraise, chiefly in the poems which make up the massive *Canto general* (1950) in which he sang the past, the present and the future of his continent—with a proliferation of highly-charged and deeply emotive symbols. Cardenal learnt part, but only a small part, of his mature technique from the way in which Neruda treated Latin American themes.

Cardenal is probably the best committed poet in the generation following that of Neruda. Most, though not all, of his poems show a sense of social involvement, but it generally works more obliquely than in the overtly social areas of Neruda's writing. The indirectness of the greater part of Cardenal's social criticism keeps at bay the stridency which mars much protest poetry —perhaps the stridency of most of Neruda's Spanish Civil War poems, for instance, links them too closely to the immediate context of that struggle for them to remain effective. Through that particular struggle, however, Neruda both learnt his trade as social poet and gained a wider kind of commitment to suffering humanity at large: a broadly humanitarian ethic shaped by, and contained within, the framework of a specifically Communist ideology. Cardenal's approach has a different ideological basis and a different tone, though both poets do have many social enemies in common.

Unlike that of Neruda, Cardenal's commitment has been specifically Christian for the greater part of his career—by which I do not mean that he preaches a Christian sermon, but that his are always Christian eyes. That was in some measure true even before his religious conversion, which took place in 1956. Nine years of training followed before his ordination in August 1965, within months of which he settled in Solentiname. The particular brand of revolutionary Christianity which he has preached and practised there, over the years, exerts great influence today among progressive Catholics in many parts of Latin America. But his poetry speaks even more strongly, and to a wider public, saying something which rings true to many people who in no sense share his religious faith.

Although his poetry is greatly admired not only throughout Latin America but in the United States and in continental Europe, it is still little-known in Britain. The aim of this anthology is to present a translation of representative poems from different phases of his writing, arranged for the most part in chronological order. The poems should, of course, be read quite independently. This introduction is intended to provide a biographical and critical context, which may help to deepen the reader's understanding afterwards.

Cardenal's poetry falls into two main periods: before and after his spiritual conversion. Both contain much that is of interest, and much that is highly original when seen in the context of the Latin American tradition. Like that of most poets, his earliest verse was highly derivative, and Darío and Neruda loom very large in the adolescent poems he wrote at school in Nicaragua and during his student years in Mexico City from 1943 to 1947: but he now rejects this stage entirely, and it is unrepresented here. What enabled him to break with the weight of this tradition was something rather unexpected in a Spanish American context: sustained contact with poetry in the English language in the United States, and in particular the poetry of Ezra Pound.

Cardenal sees Pound as the greatest single influence on his techniques, yet his poetry is not in any sense a slavish imitation of Pound. What has happened is that the impact of Pound on Cardenal's inherited Spanish American tradition has led to its renewal, much as the impact of Italian Renaissance poetry on Garcilaso led to the renewal of Spanish peninsular poetry in the sixteenth century, and there is a fine confluence of the two poetics in Cardenal's best poems. The presence of this English-language background helps to make his poetry accessible to English-speaking readers: many of its terms of reference and manners of proceeding are familiar, which helps the assimilation of its alien features, and there is also a strong streak of English common sense running through the tropical exuberance of Cardenal's indigenous inheritance.

Cardenal came under Pound's influence when he went to study in New York, at the University of Columbia, from 1947 to 1949. Pound was not the only American poet whom he read: he later collaborated with an older Nicaraguan writer, José Coronel Urtecho, to produce the standard Spanish anthology of American poetry in translation (*Antología de la poesía norteamericana*, Madrid 1963), and in 1961 he published a volume of his own translations of poems by Thomas Merton. But Merton—later his spiritual mentor—exerted no influence on the techniques of his verse, unlike Pound, whose influence has shown itself in various ways at different times. Two Poundian features have indeed remained present throughout almost all the poetry which Cardenal is willing to see kept in print, the earliest of which dates from his two years in New York.

The first of these features is an extreme cult of poetic objectivity: a conscious and deliberate suppression of subjective elements. That is to some extent characteristic of the Nicaraguan poets of Cardenal's generation, but it takes on an added degree of austerity in his case. In Cardenal's hands, verse acquires such a disciplined stress on the function of communicating through externals that Coronel Urtecho and he coined a new label for this general approach, in the mid-nineteen-fifties: they called it *exteriorismo*. It is Cardenal's pre-*exteriorista* poetry that he has chosen to discard, and all he is still willing to republish is really *exteriorista*, even if his earliest poetry in this vein predates the actual label.

The second almost constant Poundian feature is the tendency to use a documentary source: the presence of a written intermediary somewhere between the poetry itself and the experience which links it to observed reality. Such sources are usually in prose—chronicles, historical documents, anthropological reports, even newspaper articles—but this material has always been meticulously re-worked into poetry. "Omagua", the first poem in this collection (written in New York and based on a Spanish chronicle of the exploration of the Americas) shows this process at work at a rather elementary stage.

Sometimes, part of the meaning of his poems lies in their interaction with their sources, familiarity with which on the part of the reader can be presupposed (as in a later sequence of updated psalms, or in "Apocalypse"). Sometimes, one's appreciation of a poem is heightened if one happens to recognize the model. Thus "Childhood in León" has close verbal echoes of Darío's prose autobiography, and if one knows this it becomes apparent that the poem is not just about Cardenal's own childhood. In suggesting the close parallels between his childhood and Darío's, he is implicitly asking those "in the know" to compare the very different poets into which those two Nicaraguan small boys grew up. But if one does not know about the source, one is still left with a straightforward *exteriorista* account of a childhood environment, deliberately prosaic in its sobriety of statement.

At other times, as in the longer historical poems, quotations are quite explicit (often with the sources named). Occasionally one would not suspect the existence of a source at all, but there is almost always some kind of written antecedent, even in such a tropical vignette as "Above the Rain-Soaked Track". This very early poem, as yet without a social relevance, looks like personal observation, but it was inspired by a descriptive passage in a traveller's account which has been telescoped and carefully reshaped until it makes the precise points the poet wanted to communicate. Its sensuous but quiet response to tropical existence is characteristic of Cardenal's work (and displays one of his most obviously "poetic" moods), as are the studied economy of statement and the careful use of minor unobtrusive echoes as a means of patterning the structure.

His earliest committed poetry was very different. While in New York, he had been much impressed by Pound's translations from the Classics, and soon after his return to Nicaragua in 1950 he started to write epigrams himself. The earliest were amatory, then—as he began to get more deeply involved in revolutionary plotting—they turned political. At about the same time, he became engrossed in translating the Latin epigrammatists, and the first edition of the *Epigramas* (not published until 1961) contained thirty-four versions of Catullus and thirty-nine of Martial, together with the "Imitation of Propertius" and forty-eight entirely original pieces. His translations relate to their originals very much like Pound's: there is the same combination of modern distancing, which allows the poet to view the source-poem clearly, with a curious feeling of contemporaneity which establishes an often drily witty dialogue between the ancient and the modern poet.

Besides the "Imitation of Propertius", this collection includes fourteen of the original epigrams. Six are amatory (II, XII, XVI, XLVII, XLVIII, XLIX), starting with the lightly ironical "When with me, Claudia, watch how you behave". Two are non-political satires (XIV and XV), though the first of these is a dig at the money-grubbing which later became one of the main targets of Cardenal's social criticism. The other six are political, and such pieces were anonymous, circulating clandestinely, as he described in "Our poems cannot be published yet" (XXXV).

Ever since the American marines had withdrawn in 1932, Nicaragua had been virtually a police-state run by Anastasio

("Tacho") Somoza, a dictator who established something very close to a dynastic tyranny. His cynical arrogance towards his subjects is cruelly parodied in the abrasive "Somoza unveils the statue of Somoza in Somoza Stadium" (XXXI). With the dictator lauded as "Protector of the People" and "Paladin of American Democracy" in the government press, Cardenal saw the social duty of poets not merely as that of acting as the gadflies of the body-politic but also as what the young Ezra Pound—writing in 1912—grandiloquently called being "conservators of the public speech" ("The Wisdom of Poetry", *Forum*, April 1912). Cardenal put this deftly in XLI; "That is why we poets polish poems with such care / That is why my love-poems are important." Neatly turned, yet not without a touch of the adolescent arrogance that flavours Pound's obtrusive Latinism.

Reacting against the repressive character of the régime, Cardenal joined an illegal group called UNAP (Unidad Nacional de Acción Popular), becoming involved in a far-reaching plot later known as the "Conspiración de Abril". An assault on the presidential palace in Managua was planned for the night of April 3rd 1954, but someone betrayed the plot to the Guardia Nacional. Cardenal himself only just succeeded in avoiding arrest, but most of the main leaders were captured, interrogated under torture, and killed. Epigram XXX is an epitaph for the unknown grave of one of these, who simply "disappeared" in custody; the resurrection motif, here barely stated, later becomes one of Cardenal's favourite themes, endowed with multiple meanings: but now the dying that heralds a new life is given only a political and revolutionary relevance.

The feel of the times is starkly captured in XIX, a glimpse of Managua by night when the Death Squads were out. But perhaps the most revealing sign of the times is the simple fact that when the newspaper *La Prensa* published XXIX (which deals overtly solely with the peacefulness of life in neighbouring Costa Rica), the small jab of criticism implied by saying the Costa-Rican president could "go on foot in San José"—unlike the

Nicaraguan dictator in Managua—brought an angry order from Somoza for Ernesto Cardenal's arrest, and the poet had to go into hiding again until that storm blew over.

From 1954 to 1956 Cardenal worked on a much longer revolutionary poem called "Zero Hour" (*La Hora O*) whose three main episodes—not given here—dealt with United States commercial and political interference in Central America, with Sandino's guerrilla campaign against the American marines, and with the "Conspiración de Abril". The last section to be written was the brief prologue I have included, whose ending ("Watchman, what of the night?" twice over) is, as far as I know, Cardenal's first poetic use of biblical material. Technically, "Zero Hour" greatly extended his poetic range, and did so largely by incorporating two more Poundian devices: cross-cutting from source to source for startling juxtapositions, and deliberate use of flat and prosaic passages which are made to stand in abrupt contrast with lyrical evocations of landscape beauty and with the heightened epic treatment of heroic figures. "Zero Hour" is today regarded as a major Latin American revolutionary classic.

Two things of importance to Cardenal happened in the year in which he finished "Zero Hour". Firstly, Somoza was finally assassinated by a poet. Though Cardenal was not involved, he was fortunate to escape the instant wave of police reprisals. Secondly, Cardenal experienced a far-reaching spiritual crisis, which led him to renounce all forms of violence and apply for admission to the novitiate of the Trappist monastery of Gethsemani, in Kentucky. Thomas Merton, whose early writings had already impressed the poet as a student in New York, was novice-master at Gethsemani. With the experience of coming under his tutelage, Merton became the dominant influence both on Cardenal's spiritual life and on his way of viewing social problems. In the specific context of non-violence, Cardenal always names Merton and Gandhi jointly as his models.

One of the last poems he wrote before he left the tropics for Kentucky was "NNW", in which the rebirth of the species (transcending individual lives) picks up the resurrection theme in different terms. Literary allusions throng behind his response to natural phenomena, and the concluding stress on the urgency which drives migrating creatures on, echoes the almost instinctual purposiveness behind his own migration northwards.

Cardenal's vocation to the priesthood was a late one. He was already thirty-two when he reached the novitiate, in May 1957. His career as an ordinand was, furthermore, twice interrupted. Ill-health forced him to leave the Trappists two years later, and in August 1959 he moved to the Benedictine community at Cuernavaca, in Mexico, to continue his studies in a monastic setting although he did not wish to join the order itself. His plans to found an independent community which would practise a more primitive form of Christian living were already well-advanced. Early in 1961, he moved on to the seminary of La Ceja (near Medellín, in Colombia) where he completed his training for the priesthood. He was forty-one by the time he returned to Nicaragua some days before his ordination, which took place in Managua on August 15th 1965, the Feast of the Assumption. Preparations for settling at Solentiname took several months, and he arrived there on February 16th 1966 with two companions, to begin clearing the land before the rainy season.

Much had happened to his thought and writings in the nine years since his conversion. During the first phase—his two years at Gethsemani—he composed no poetry, as all secular writing was discouraged during the novitiate. But he kept a notebook of loosely structured prose meditations, on the theme of love as the matrix of existence, and these formed the basis of a book of spiritual reflections which he completed at Cuernavaca. It was only published in 1970, as *Vida en el amor* (English translation, *Love*, London, 1974), though Merton's preface was signed as early as January 1966. Its inspiration goes back to the Christian neo-Platonism of Augustine and the early Fathers of the Church, but its lyrical vision of a universe formed by the outpouring of God's love is Franciscan in its simplicity and in its sense of spiritual happiness. The Rhineland and the Spanish mystics (especially St John of the Cross) contributed to its approach and attitudes. There is also some influence of Teilhard de Chardin, but there is a joyously naive enthusiasm about the work which is entirely Cardenal's.

Whereas his poetry is usually self-explanatory, many aspects of his later poems—and particularly the nature of his response to primitive peace-loving myths ("Tahirassawichi in Washington", for example, in this collection)—make deeper sense when they are read again in the light of this extended interpretation of the nature of existence. It also underlies his own particular vision of the final stage of evolution, at the end of "Apocalypse" (which, though figurative, is perhaps meant more literally than one might imagine). His reading of St John of the Cross provides the mystical opening and end of "Night", forming a framework of deep peace inside which his critique of the restlessness of modern "culture" falls logically into place. One has, in short, to turn to *Love* to appreciate the fuller meaning of Cardenal's peculiarly intimate perspective on both the universe and man's affairs.

Although he wrote no poetry at Gethsemani, stray jottings were later polished into thirty-one tightly disciplined small poems at Cuernavaca, published in 1960 under the title *Gethsemani, Kentucky*. In his preface, Merton described them as sketches in the style of the T'ang dynasty, in which the whole effect is achieved by a few deft strokes of the brush. Five of these poems are given here. "Jet at evening" consists of only five quick, isolated phrases. "Behind the monastery" provides a treatment of the resurrection theme in seemingly incongruous terms. Others, such as "In the woods", record the fascination of a frozen winter. But it was the shift from northern winter towards spring that most moved Cardenal (accustomed to the tropical alternation between arid heat and humid heat) and in "The marmots are not dead" the sleep of hibernating animals and their "rebirth" in spring become a "figure" of the Resurrection—the more effective for not being spelt out. The sense of quickening life which fills that poem moves into the steady rhythm of the agricultural year, in "A hum of tractors". Such simple poems conceal a richness of thought which only becomes apparent if they are read in the light of *Love*, when each falls into place as part of a sensitive and unified world-picture. But a large part of their virtue as poems lies in the fact that they leave their spiritual message unstated—almost enigmatic. Cardenal took this technique of understatement over into his specifically social poetry as well.

After the restraint of Gethsemani, his shorter period at Cuernavaca proved very fruitful. Besides writing up *Gethsemani* and giving final shape to *Love*, he saw *La Hora O* and the *Epigrams* into print, translated a collection of Merton's poems into Spanish (Thomas Merton, *Poemas*, Mexico, 1961), and wrote a number of shorter pieces such as "Vale of Cuernavaca" and "On Lake Nicaragua". He also carried out a major piece of "historico-poetical" research, chiefly in the anthropological and historical sections of the library of the Museo Nacional de México. This resulted in *El estrecho dudoso* ("The Doubtful Passage"), whose title refers to the non-existent straits between the Atlantic and Pacific which the early *conquistadores* sought in Central America —and which they thought they had found when, on ascending the Río San Juan, they reached the great Sweet-Water Sea which was Lake Nicaragua.

El estrecho dudoso—completed during his second year at Cuernavaca but not published for five years (Madrid, 1966)— is a long and technically fascinating epic poem, in twenty-five sections, only one of which ("Destruction of Santiago de Quauhtemalan") is included here. Explicitly, this epic deals with the history of Central America from its discovery by the Spaniards to the destruction of León Viejo (the first capital of Nicaragua) by Volcán Momotombo in 1609, and it is built up by interweaving passages inspired by—or in some cases taken directly from—early chronicles, accounts of early explorations, and actual documents to be found in the archives of the period. Indirectly, the material becomes an oblique commentary on multiple aspects of the modern period. Thus Pedrarias ("El Muy Magnífico Señor Pedrarias Dávila/*Furor Domini!*"), who was the first "exploiter" of Nicaragua—the first "promoter of commerce" and importer of slaves—is used as a "figure" of Somoza and, through him, of all tyrannical dictators.

The mass of documentary material which lies behind the poetic text is carefully reworked, with much cross-cutting from one level of implication to another as well as from source to source, following the manner of Pound's *Cantos*. As in the *Cantos*, the free-verse sequences are made acceptable as poetry by a concentration upon direct treatment of the "surface" subject, a careful stripping away of inessential words, and a rhythmical articulation of the text into a steady ebb-and-flow of sounding phrases. Although in technique Pound's *Cantos* were the model, Cardenal's historical vision is more like that of Neruda's *Canto general*; but he has added the specifically Christian—almost Providentialist—dimension which gives spiritual depth to nearly all his later poems on socio-political topics.

The themes of savagery and greed, but also those of high adventure and dedicated spirits, recur continually; the episodes reinforce one another as the tale develops, and the entire human action is played out against a backdrop of the beauty and terror of the tropics. Given the close interdependence of the parts, it is hard to represent the poem faithfully by any extract, but the one I have chosen stands out as an account of the shattering destructiveness of natural forces, narrated in the spare style of the contemporary chronicler. It describes the destruction of the first capital, today called Ciudad Vieja, of what is now Guatemala ("Quauhtemalan") in 1541; the second, Antigua, was wrecked by an earthquake in 1773; and Guatemala City—the present capital—was almost completely destroyed early this century.

Ernesto Cardenal also wrote his first poem on a pre-Columbian theme at Cuernavaca. "Lost Cities" began a line of thought he has pursued, intermittently, ever since, namely the treatment of the Indian past of the Americas (and, later, that of primitive communities which still survive) in such a way that the evocation of a distant way of life becomes by implication a critique of the patterns of conduct, the values, and the modes of thought of modern capitalist societies. Most of the poems written in this vein were brought together in 1969 in *Homenaje a los indios americanos*; an expanded version was published in Chile in the following year and was reprinted in Argentina in 1972 (English translation: *Homage to the American Indians*, Baltimore, 1973). Given the importance of this group of poems, the first example deserves closer attention.

"Lost Cities" is on a Mayan theme. It starts with wild beasts prowling through a ruined city hidden in tropical jungle —beasts once stylized in the friezes on the walls. This contrast between past and present shifts to the values of early Mayan culture, before Mexican Toltecs brought in martial arts and human sacrifice, and the early Maya are particularly praised because "There are no names of generals on the stelae" and they had "no word for *master*" nor "for *city wall*". Later, the poem turns to the Mayan cult of time, focussing on its notion of recurring cycles (called *katuns*) which would ultimately be re-enacted; after reverting to the modern jungle (a "figure" of our society), the poem ends asking whether past *katuns* will ever return—whether, in other words, culture can ever again be grounded on a selflessly religious cult of peace.

The poem depends on serious archaeological works, but it was directly inspired by an article about Tikal cut out of *Life* and pinned up on the novitiate noticeboard by Thomas Merton, to whom Ernesto attributes the growth of his interest in Amerindian topics. The popular source becomes both an intermediary between past and present, and—perhaps more reliably—a means of conveying a message concerning the present in terms of something which one takes, initially, to be a simple evocation of the past. Later poems use the same technique, but they present their elements discontinuously, and the sustained approach of "Lost Cities" lets one appreciate the basic play of attitudes more easily. It was the only poem on such a theme composed at Cuernavaca.

Cardenal did not immediately resume this type of composition in La Ceja. Two completely different kinds of subject occupied him first. The one involved meditation on some event or on some aspect of contemporary life—one poem was based on the report of an air-crash (again read in *Life*), another on tourist propaganda, and yet another on gangster killings. In each case, the insecurity and falsity of modern life led to an implied (and sometimes an explicit) criticism of the values underlying the affluent society typified by the United States, values reflected most clearly in the ethos of the glossy advertisements in *Life* or the *New Yorker*. Some of these poems had been written at Cuernavaca, but the best-known (though, to my mind, not his best composition in this vein) is "Prayer for Marilyn Monroe", composed in Colombia, which gave its name to a slim collection (*Oración por Marilyn Monroe y otros poemas*) published in Medellín in 1965.

Perhaps the best of these poems, "Night", came considerably later, when he had already been some time at Solentiname. It was an unexpected interlude in the composition of the main sequence of long poems in *Homage to the American Indians*. Bringing together the most interesting aspects of his poetic vision and techniques, including cross-cutting and collage (by then both dominant features), this long poem starts and ends with mystical passages. Between them, comes a discontinuous sequence of images indicting aspects of modern American society: its values, as reflected in *New Yorker* advertisements (whose English-language slogans, in block capitals, intrude into the rhythms of the

Spanish verse); its big-business incentives and rewards; the threat of war and violence projected into one's own home on television; juvenile delinquency, drop-out philosophies, and the desperate loneliness at the heart of city-life. His indictment is a searing one. The quietly reiterating rhythms of the mystical conclusion bring a smoothing out of those abrasive angularities, and the last line is possibly one of the best he has ever written: "La música callada no es de cuerdas de Nylon" ("The silent music is not played on nylon strings").

The other interest developed in La Ceja also began in Mexico, with "Unrighteous Mammon", a poem prompted by a sermon on Luke 16. 9 preached by the Benedictine prior. That series of reflections on a scriptural text, seeking its modern relevance, meshed with something which began not as a poetic device but as a devotional exercise. At Gethsemani, Cardenal had been brought into continual contact with the psalms, whose reading, in Latin, formed the major part of the canonical hours—the backbone of communal monastic prayer. He found the only way to make them personally meaningful was to transpose them inwardly—while saying them—to fit the circumstances of the modern world, whose different joys and terrors (rightly seen) all had their parallels in those of the Old Testament. Such a process of mental adjustment brought the psalms "back to life" for him, and the interplay of meaning between the old and the new deepened his experience of both.

In La Ceja, he used this devotional technique to write a sequence of twenty-five "up-dated" psalms (first published in the *Revista de la Universidad de Antioquia*, Medellín, 1964). Each keeps the number of its biblical model, and the interplay between two different levels of historical experience (which underlines the enduring likenesses between them) is reinforced on the linguistic plane—in Cardenal's originals—by the continuous ebb-and-flow of associations between the Latin of the Vulgate Bible and the terms and rhythms of twentieth-century Spanish (itself a highly Latinate tongue). In the five versions included here, I have tried to achieve a similar effect by exploiting what I take to be our latent cultural familiarity with Coverdale's version of the psalms, as used liturgically for centuries in the Book of Common Prayer. Although there may be no close knowledge of those texts amongst most readers today, perhaps there are still enough echoes of the phraseology in their experience of the English language for the "matching process" still to have some of the intended impact.

Whereas most of Cardenal's previous poetry was born of either his American or his Latin American reading and experience, and his conscience as a committed individual was moved primarily by the plight of people in his own continent, exploration of the psalms extended his range of sympathies to the sufferings of all mankind—in the concentration camps of World War II, in bombed Hiroshima, in hospital wards and lunatic asylums, in homes for the aged, and not only in the prison-yards and torture-chambers of countries like Brazil or Nicaragua. Though not all his psalms are equally successful as poetry, they are by far the most widely-known (and certainly the most translated) of his works, and the best of them have stood the test of liturgical use in Latin America. But this mode of composition had its perils, and most of what the poet wanted to express through this device had been sufficiently conveyed by the end of that sequence.

One general moral remained unstated. Those were the days of worldwide fears of a nuclear holocaust (a possibility as real as ever, of course, but one with which we have—perhaps presumptuously—now learnt to live), and Cardenal put his own thoughts on this subject into words in "Apocalypse", employing the same technique of meshing modern terms of reference with a scriptural source: the Apocalypse or Book of Revelation of St John the Divine. The immediate drive for "Apocalypse", which is his longest biblical poem, came from *Breakthrough to Peace* (New York, 1962), edited by Merton, and in particular from one of its twelve essays entitled "What Would It Really Be Like? An H-

Bomb on New York City", by Tom Stonier, which provided many circumstantial details. The vision of the power-blocks of the East and West as Gog and Magog was inspired by Merton's "A letter to Pablo Antonio Cuadra concerning giants" (*Emblems of a Season of Fury*, 1961), whilst the enigmatic evocation of an ultimate New Earth grows out of the concluding sections of *Love*.

During his years in La Ceja, Cardenal's interest in the Amerindian past and present of his continent steadily increased. He twice visited the Cuna Indians (once those in Panamanian territory and once the branch of the tribe living in Colombia). He also travelled in the Upper Amazon basin, and began working intensively in the anthropological collections of libraries in Medellín and Bogotá. One of the projects he had in mind was a prose study of the religious and mystical beliefs of primitive people, emphasizing parallels between primitive and Christian rituals. This plan was later abandoned, largely because he thought its close attention to ritual was irrelevant to the way the post-conciliar Church was moving. Instead, his anthropological readings, and the drafts of many chapters of this abandoned book, became the source-material of many poems included in *Homage to the American Indians*. Two of its longer poems—"Cantares Mexicanos (I)", included here, and "Nele de Kantule"—were written in Colombia, and another, "The Economy of Tahuantinsuyu", was begun—though it was completed in Nicaragua in December 1965. With these three Amerindian poems, the area of reference widened.

It widened further still when, after his ordination in Managua, Ernesto Cardenal was finally able to settle in Solentiname on Mancarrón, clear his own land, build his own hut, and begin a life in which hard manual labour, contemplation, care of souls, scholarship, and the writing of his poetry could be combined exactly as he chose, fulfilling the ideal plan he had worked out with Merton's guidance years before. The expansion of his Amerindian interests followed a clear pattern, moving from the high pre-Columbian civilizations to more primitive cultures.

"Lost Cities" had been on a Mayan theme, and there were to be several other Mayan poems, including "Katun 11 Ahau", which appears in this anthology. Three more poems derive directly or indirectly, from the highly cultured legacy of ancient Mexican poetry, chiefly known to Cardenal through León-Portilla's Spanish versions: the title of "Cantares Mexicanos (1)", the first Amerindian poem written at La Ceja, is an allusion to a famous codex of Nahuatl poems. The third main area of immediately pre-Columbian culture, that of the Inca empire, provides the example of a moneyless economy which in "Economy of Tahuantisuyu" (the name means the land of the four horizons) he praises so highly in contrast to the profit-oriented systems of today. But he was not blind to its totalitarian characteristics. The second Amerindian poem written in Colombia, "Nele de Kantule" (not included here), dealt with a strictly primitive community, that of the Panamanian Cuna Indians whom he had visited. Later, as his own "primitive" Christian community developed, his increasing interest in the beliefs of non-Christian primitive cultures was reflected in a number of poems on North American "Red Indian" themes.

In the time between his ordination and the move to Solentiname, he had gone to see Merton (for guidance in the matter of his foundation) and had also visited the surviving culture of the Puebla Indians in New Mexico—an experience he found profoundly moving. The anthropological literature on the Red Indian cultures was copious, he found many aspects of their beliefs and symbolism rich in implications, and the contrast between the values of these cultures and those of the "modern" civilization which had supplanted them (and in most cases utterly destroyed them) supplied fresh openings for implicit criticism of modern "Western" man. The only Red Indian poem included here, "Tahirassawichi in Washington", shows this at its best. The deliberately prosaic note of its throwaway final comment, which implies so much, leaves one with a feeling of total breakdown in communication not just between two cultures but between two "systems" which neither have, nor could ever have, anything in common.

In the values these poems expound, and the motivations they discover behind the multiple symbolic aspects of the cultures they examine, there is always the same oblique attack on modern socio-economic structures, on all forms of exploitation, and on that cult of militarism whose absence had struck him as the noblest feature of the early Maya in "Lost Cities". Since that first treatment of such themes, however, these poems have become progressively more intricate in structure. Their occasional descriptive passages are extremely emotive, despite *exteriorista* objectivity, but the primary device used to achieve an impact on the reader is a cinematographic sequence of discontinuous images. Their calculated programme of effects has been built up, like that of a film, in the "cutting-room", when (at the stage of various successive drafts) the poet tries out different sequences for the constituent imagistic parts, each of which is a separate and discrete unit. A comparison between the steady flow of "Lost Cities" and the interrupted sequence of "Katun ll Ahau", whose staccato rhythms impose pauses of both different qualities and different lengths upon the reader, shows how the imagistic and linguistic texture has changed. "Katun 11 Ahau" also makes a different use of Mayan material. Its title, the name of a particular cycle in the Mayan calendar, denotes a period of general disaster and distress, and instead of evoking a past golden age to contrast with our own, this poem invokes the terminology of the *Chilam Balam* (the Mayan sacred book) to characterize the evils of the age in which we live.

In the nature of cyclic time, this age must pass, and Cardenal also presents his hopes for a new future in Mayan terms. It is to be a Christian future, when the "Katun of the Tree of Life shall be established", and the achievement of social justice will produce the *katun* called "Union-for-a-Common-Cause" when we shall no longer "have to keep our voices low". At the end of each period of time, the Mayan temples were rebuilt, not demolishing the earlier ones but enclosing the old pyramids in larger and better ones, representing a later and more developed stage of Mayan art: and in the evils of the present age the priest or *chilan*—"he that is mouth"—perceives the portents of a coming change: "It is the time for building the new pyramids / upon the basis of the old." The same message had been given in biblical terms at the end of Psalm 22: "There will be a banquet set before those that are poor. / And there shall be a great feast among our people: / the new people, that is to be born."

Such a future is not intangible: its values already exist and motivate a way of life at Nuestra Señora de Solentiname. In "Katun 11 Ahau", it is no accident that the *chilan* plays such a prominent part in the life of his society. I think this is the rôle which Ernesto Cardenal has set aside for the modern poet-priest, as the initiator of social change, and he sees his poetry as carrying ill tidings to the tyrants of our age. He is himself the poet-priest who "delivers tablets which predict eclipses".

What this means in concrete terms is another matter. It is easy to set up a viable commune, but to set up a Latin American republic whose structures are really grounded in social justice is something very different. In 1970 Cardenal spent three months in Castro's Cuba. He was far from blind to many shortcomings of the new system, and yet he was persuaded that many things which he had previously considered unattainable this century could indeed be put into practice, given such radical changes in the social order. All the Cuban system seemed to lack to become a viable replacement for the western society whose values and abuses he had so long deplored was a Christian dimension. Cuba simply lacked the firm grounding of that which was done here-and-now in principles which looked beyond this time-bound world towards a timeless reality, from which they might take their being and in which would lie their strength.

His Cuban experience was, as he once said to me, almost "a second conversion", and he came back convinced that the form of primitive Christian society which he had brought into being in miniature, in Solentiname, could be "writ large" given the right promotion of awareness. This "promotion of awareness" is the process of conscientization—an awkward word in English, perhaps, but one frequently used in the literature of the new Latin American Catholicism and of the "theology of liberation" movement. Somewhere in all this, however, Cardenal's old ideal of strict non-violence had become qualified. Recognizing that Latin American society is unlikely to be successfully restructured without recourse to arms, his Christianity has become more militantly revolutionary of late. One of his recent longer poems (not in this volume) is even dedicated to the urban guerrilla movement in Nicaragua : the Frente Sandinista de Liberación Nacional, named after the guerrilla leader who defied the American marines from 1926 to 1932. One must wait for a new book in prose for a proper statement of Cardenal's own social programme now, although the title of a volume of interviews he gave in 1972—*On the Sanctity of Revolution* (*Von der Heiligkeit der Revolution*, Wuppertal, 1973)—shows the way his thought is tending.

Since his return from Cuba, Cardenal's poetry has changed in a number of ways, in content and in style, but that is another story. This volume ends with the last long poem he wrote before that journey, and it is arguably the finest poem he has yet written. It is his elegy on the death of Thomas Merton, who died in Bangkok on December 10th 1968—accidentally killed when he put out his hand to adjust an electric fan with faulty wiring. Cardenal has always regarded Thomas Merton as the guiding spirit behind his commune at Solentiname, although Merton had never been there : it had never proved "practical" to go (as the poem says, quoting one of his letters), though such a visit had been planned for after his return from Asia.

Cardenal's lament, which is at the same time a poem full of rejoicing, is extremely complex. It makes use of almost every technique he had ever employed, and brings in an immense variety of references: religious reading at Gethsemani, the Classics, Chinese poetry, the beliefs of primitive people regarding death and the after-life, contemporary events (that was the Christmastide of the first moon landing), phrases quoted in English (these are italicized in my translation), advertisements which he could not help reading in a figurative sense ("Advertisements are manuals of meditation, says Corita . . . Don't take them at face value"), and finally the personal recollections we can glimpse behind so many names and phrases.

Behind the whole poem there is, moreover, one constant literary reference: the very title ("Coplas a la muerte de Merton") echoes that of the most famous elegy in the Spanish language, the fifteenth-century "Coplas por la muerte de su padre" of Jorge Manrique. Manrique's opening lines ("Our lives are the rivers that run down into the sea, which is death") resound insistently behind the first lines of Cardenal's poem in the original Spanish: "Nuestras vidas son los ríos/que van a dar a la muerte/que es la vida" ("Our lives are the rivers which run down into the death that is life" would be a literal rendering). The whole poem is a series of variations on that one fundamental inversion of one of the best-known quotations in all Spanish literature. Additional small twists are given to it, every now and again, and there are sudden allusive echoes of its insistent rhythmic phrases. It is as though an English poet had taken up the challenge of composing a long poem aimed at turning "To be or not to be, that is the question" inside out, and building up the statement of a whole philosophy on its reversal.

In the Spanish text, the Manrique is never used directly, but it acts as the sounding-board for every statement made. Rightly or wrongly, I persuaded Cardenal to let me state his own unstated premiss in my version, in order to allow the English reader to take off—so to speak—on the right foot: "Manrique said our lives were rivers/going down to the sea which is death/but the death they flow down to is life". (That is the only major liberty which I have taken anywhere in this collection.) With the other references in this poem, whereas spotting sources may provide intellectual satisfaction, not knowing them is no barrier to understanding what it is intended to convey. Full of its own internal echoes, it is a poem which works in a deliberately elusive and allusive way, by means of tantalizing glimpses and suggestions, cutting from one half-insight to the next—the splicing showing Cardenal's mastery of a technique which could so easily simply be disconcerting, but is used here to construct a deftly modulated flow of images that add up, finally, to harmony and peace.

Thomas Merton's death marked the end of a period in the life of Cardenal, and "Death of Thomas Merton" marks the culmination of a period in his poetry. Although that poetry may be firmly Spanish American, it has things to say to all of us which are important, and which could perhaps only be said to us with authority today by someone speaking with a Third-World voice.

St Catherine's College,
Oxford, 1974 *Robert Pring-Mill*

Omagua

For the great things Captain Orellana said that he had seen.
For the great things Captain Orellana said that he had seen.
Such things were told of the great river and the neighbouring lands
and in particular of the province called Omagua,
                that we set out to search for this Omagua.
Coasting the flat land running inwards almost from the shore
halting at the hour of vespers every night
the men would land to hunt for mussels and go fishing
once two men went in search of food together
and did not return
nor did we ever know what happened to them.
We met many Indians on the river in canoes
and always shouted asking for Omagua.
Omagua. Omagua.
Orsúa said : that those
who started out as youths would be grey-haired . . .
The men were dying of hunger in that watery waste.
We covered seven hundred leagues and no Omagua.
Omagua. Omagua.
What hopes the land which bore that name had raised !
One evening, in a village of great circular huts
palm-thatched right to the ground, some days
before Orsúa was killed amongst the cooking-pots,
Núñez de Guevara, strolling to relieve the great heat of the night,

saw a shadow slipping by the palisade, crying :
"Pedro de Orsúa, Governor of El Dorado and Omagua,
may God have mercy on your soul !"
And said he pursued the shadow in the darkness
but there was no one there.

Above the rain-soaked track

Above the rain-soaked track down which the girls with jars
came and went,
             on steps cut in the rock,
hung great lianas from the trees
like heads of hair or snakes.
There was a superstitious feeling in the air.
Below :
         the lemon-hued lagoon,
                    like polished jade.
Cries would rise from the water
and the sound of mud-coloured bodies plunging into water.
            A superstitious feeling . . .
The girls who came and went, with jars,
sang an old love-song as they passed.
Those who came up, erect as statues :
beneath their wet red amphorae with painted patterns,
         wet bodies, with the shape of amphorae.
And those who went down
          went prancing and dancing, leapt like deer,
their skirts unfolding in the wind like flowers.

Childhood in León

I lived in a large house by the Church of St Francis
                with AVE MARIA
inscribed in the entrance hall,
red-floored passages of baked mud-bricks,
and old red tiles,
                windows with rusty iron grilles,
a large patio heavy in the airless afternoon,
one of those birds which sadly sounds the hours,
and the white image of an aunt saying the rosary
                down in the patio.
As evening came one heard the bells for the Angelus
                ("The Angel of the Lord said unto Mary...")
notes struck on a distant piano by some girl
                and the bugle down in the barracks.
At night, a huge red moon above the Church of Calvary.
And I was told tales of ghosts and souls in torment:
                at midnight
General Arechabala's shade rode through the streets.
And the creak of a door, shutting... A black coach...
An empty cart rattles along the Calle Real.
And, some time later, the cocks of the neighbourhood crowing
and the calls of the clock-bird,
and my aunt going daily out to Mass at 4 am
with the bells ringing
                in St Francis, ringing
in Calvary,

                        and in the Hospice of St John
and the metal jars of the milkmen bumping along the stones
and a seller of bread, knocking on the door of the hall
and calling
    BREAD
        BREAD . . .

Watch how you behave

When with me, Claudia, watch how you behave :
your slightest gesture, word, or sigh—
yes, Claudia's slightest slip—
may meet the scrutiny of learned men one day,
and this dance, Claudia, be recalled for centuries.

Claudia : you have been warned !

(Epigram II)

Costa-Rican roses

Accept these Costa-Rican roses, Miriam,
with a song to tell my love. Its lines
are to remind you that each rose's face
is like your face; the roses
are to remind you love gets cut like them
and that your face will pass like Greece or Rome.
When there is no more love, no Costa-Rican roses,
then, Miriam, you'll think of this sad song.

(Epigram XII)

Imitation of Propertius

I do not sing of the defence of Stalingrad
nor of the desert war
nor the landings in Sicily
nor yet of Eisenhower crossing the Rhine.

I only sing the conquest of a girl.

Nor was it with gems from Joyería Morlock
nor Dreyfus perfumes
nor yet with orchids in their perspex case
nor with a Cadillac
but only with my poems that I conquered her.

And she prefers me, poor, to all Somoza's millions.

(Epigram XIII)

For twenty years

You strove for twenty years
to get together twenty million pesos
but we'd give twenty million pesos
not to strive as you have striven.

(Epigram XIV)

You?

You?
You don't deserve an epigram.

(Epigram XV)

That street with yellow lights

I still recall that street with yellow lights
and that full moon among the criss-cross wires
and that star at the corner of the street,
a radio playing a long way off,
eleven striking from the tower of La Merced that night,
and in that street : the gold light of your open door.

(Epigram XVI)

Shots last night

Some shots were heard last night.
Down by the cemetery.
No one knows whom they killed—Or how many.
No one knows anything.
Some shots were heard last night.
And that is all.

(Epigram XIX)

Carters sing

In Costa Rica, carters sing.
Men on the roads with mandolins.
And ox-carts bright as parrots.
And oxen with coloured ribbons,
bells, and flowers on their horns.

At coffee-harvest time in Costa Rica.
When all carts are heaped high with coffee beans.

And bands play in village squares
and the windows and the balconies of San José
are full of girls and full of flowers.
And girls there go for walks in parks.
And the President can go on foot in San José.

(Epigram XXIX)

Epitaph for Adolfo Báez Bone

They killed you. Never said where they had buried you.
Since then our land itself has been your grave. Or, rather :
wherever you were never laid to rest, you rise.

They thought they'd killed you at the order "Fire!"
They thought they'd buried you. Rather :
that which they had buried was a seed.

(Epigram XXX)

Somoza unveils the statue of Somoza in Somoza Stadium

Not that I believe that people raised this statue to me,
I know as well as you that I commissioned it.
Nor that I thereby hope for immortality :
I know the people will one day destroy it.
Nor that I wished to give myself in life
the monument you will not raise when I am dead :
but that I had it raised knowing you hate it.

(Epigram XXXI)

Our poems cannot be published

Our poems cannot be published yet.
They pass from hand to hand, in manuscript
or cyclostyled. A day will come, however,
when the name of the dictator they attack
will be forgotten,
and they will still be read.

(Epigram XXXV)

Have you not read, my love?

Have you not read, my love, in *Novedades* :
WATCHMAN OF PEACE, GENIUS OF LABOUR
PALADIN OF AMERICAN DEMOCRACY
DEFENDER OF AMERICAN CATHOLICISM
PROTECTOR OF THE PEOPLE
        THE BENEFACTOR?
They sack the people's language,
devalue the people's words.
(Just like the people's money.)
That is why we poets polish poems with great care.
That is why my love-poems are important.

(Epigram XLI)

Heavy raindrops

The heavy raindrops seem
like footsteps on the stairs
with the wind at the door like a girl
about to come in.

(Epigram XLVII)

You came in dreams

You came in dreams
but the void you left on leaving
was reality.

(Epigram XLVIII)

Nearest me

The person nearest me :
you. Whom, notwithstanding,
I've not seen for an age
except in dreams.

(Epigram XLIX)

Zero hour

Central America : tropical nights,
volcanoes and lagoons beneath the moon
and lights in presidential palaces;
barracks, and sad bugle-calls at dusk.
"I frequently decide the death of man
while smoking a cigarette"
says Ubico, smoking a cigarette...
In his palace, which is like a pink-iced cake,
Ubico has a cold. The crowd outside
has been dispersed with tear-gas bombs.
San Salvador, at night : distrust and spying,
muttering in the homes and small hotels,
and screams in police stations.
The crowd stoned the palace of Carías,
breaking just one window of his office,
but the police opened fire on the crowd.
And Managua : covered by deployed machine-guns
from its palace, which is like a chocolate cake :
steel helmets out patrolling in the streets.
> *Watchman, what of the night?*
> *Watchman, what of the night?*

NNW

When fox-cubs are born and tadpoles hatch
and the male butterfly dances in front of the female
and the king-fishers touch beaks,
and the light grows longer and ovaries swell,
the swallows will return from the South . . .
Will "return" from the South?
        "The dark swallows"
those that flew off in September to North Africa,
crowded every curving loop of wire,
darkened the afternoons,
and filled the sky with voices,
those will not return.

And the eels that swam downriver in Africa
and sought the Sargasso Sea to consummate
their nuptials clad in silver wedding garments,
like the ladies of the Court of King Don Juan:
where are they now?
      The palolos of the Southern Seas
which rise to the surface at their feast of fecundation
when the November moon is at its full
and cover the whole sea those nights with phosphorescent foam
and sink back beneath the sea not to return?

And the gilded *catopsilias* garbed like Queen Thi
migrate each autumn NNW
leaving behind the nectar, flowers, the mating

with nothing ahead save billows, salt, sea-loneliness
and death (lying NNW)
        North-North-West
but on a steady bearing NNW.

A hum of tractors

There is a hum of tractors in the fields.
The cherry-trees are pink with blossom.
And, look, the apple-trees are in full bloom.
This, Beloved, is the season of love.
The starlings sing in the sycamore.
The roads smell of fresh tar,
and passing cars bear laughing girls.
Look : the season of love has come.
Each bird that flies has one pursuing it.

Jet at evening

A jet in the evening sky,
vapour like a thread—
as the sun sets, golden.
The plane too fast to see :
the gold flight lingers.

In the woods

One would think there was a cocktail-party in the woods :
like the chink of ice-cubes in glasses,
or the clink of glass on glass as toasts are drunk,
or the tinkle of the cut-glass chandeliers,
one hears the tinkling of the woods hard held by frost—
ice clinking against ice out in the loneliness.

The marmots are not dead

The marmots in their burrows are not dead,
they sleep. Nor are the chipmunks dead,
nor have they gone away : curled up,
they lie asleep beneath the earth.
Adders sleep beneath dead leaves;
frogs, buried deep in frozen mud
down by the icebound river, also sleep.
The river sleeps as well. Life is asleep.
In caves, cracks, hollows, secret galleries,
eggs, silk cocoons, seeds, buds
all wait for spring. There are tracks in the snow :
the tracks of fox and skunk, each going out
by night, already searching for a mate.
There is a smell of skunk, these nights.

Behind the monastery

Behind the monastery, down by the road,
there is a cemetery of worn-out things
where lie smashed china, rusty metal,
cracked pipes and twisted bits of wire,
empty cigarette packets, sawdust,
corrugated iron, old plastic, tyres beyond repair :
all waiting for the Resurrection, like ourselves.

Lost cities

At night, owls fly among the stelae,
the wildcat snarls along the terraces,
the jaguar roars in towers,
a stray coyote howls in the Great Square
at the image of the moon in the lagoons
which in remote *katuns* were reservoirs.

Now, the animals are real
which in the frescoes were once stylized;
and princes now sell pots in markets.
But how can one inscribe the hieroglyph again?
Again paint jaguars, and dethrone tyrants?
Rebuild again our tropical acropolis,
our rural capitals amid the *milpa* fields?

The jungle thickets full of monuments.
Altars in *milpas*. Arches
with bas-reliefs among the buttressed roots.
In jungle where it seems man never entered,
where only the ant-eater and the tapir
and the quetzal (still garbed like a Maya) go:
there lies an entire city.
When priests went up the Temple of the Jaguar
with jaguar capes, fans of quetzal feathers,
deerskin sandals and ritual masks,
shouting went up from the Ball-Courts
with drumbeats, and the scent of copal incense

from the sacred chambers of *zapote* wood,
and the smoke of pinewood torches . . . Whilst underneath Tikal
there is another city a millennium older.
—Today the monkeys howl on the *zapote* trees.

There are no names of generals on the stelae.

In their temples and palaces and pyramids
and calendars and chronicles and codices
there is not one name of a leader, chief, or emperor,
or priest or politician or commander or governor;
nor did they record political events on monuments,
nor administrations, nor dynasties,
nor ruling families, nor political parties.
In centuries, not one glyph recording a man's name :
the archaeologists still do not know how they were governed.

Their language had no word for "master".
Nor a word for "city-wall". They did not wall their cities.
Their cities were cities of temples, they lived in the fields,
among the palm-groves and the *milpas* and the pawpaw trees.
Their temple-arch was modelled on their hut.
Highways were for processions.
Religion was the only bond between them,
but it was a religion freely accepted,
imposing no burden. No oppression.
Their priests had no temporal power
and the pyramids were built without forced labour.
At its height their civilization did not turn into an empire !
Nor had they colonies. Nor did they know the arrow.

They knew Jesus as the God of the Maize
and gave him simple offerings
of maize, of birds, of feathers.
They had no wars, nor knew the wheel,
but they had calculated the synodic path of Venus :
every night they noted the rising of Venus

on the horizon, over some distant *ceiba* tree,
as pairs of parrots flew homing to their nests.
They had no metallurgy. Their tools were of stone—
they never left the Stone Age, technologically speaking.
But they computed precise dates going back
four hundred million years into the past.
They had no applied sciences. They were not practical.
Their progress lay in religion, mathematics, art,
astronomy. They had no means of weighing.
They adored time : the mysterious
effluxion of time.
Time was holy. Days were gods.
The past and the future intermingled in their songs.
They used the same *katuns* for past and future,
in the belief that time was re-enacted
like the motions of the heavenly bodies they observed.
Yet the time which they adored abruptly ceased.
Stelae remained unfinished,
blocks half-cut in quarries—
and there they lie.

Only lonely gum-tappers traverse the Petén today.
Vampire bats nest in the stucco friezes.
Wild pigs grunt in the avenues at nightfall.
The jaguar roars in towers—towers root-entangled—,
far away in a distant square a lone coyote bays the moon,
and the Pan American jet flies high above the pyramid.
But will the past *katuns* one day return?

Vale of Cuernavaca from the Monastery

When there's been rain,
the air above the Vale is even clearer :
      the smoke of huts yet whiter
                the volcanoes a deeper blue
   the bells yet more distinct.

        A barefoot lad
        drives cattle
        down the stony track.

On the blue mountains, even bluer shadows :
      shadows of contours
or perhaps of clouds.
        (And a single small red bird
                on the telephone wire.)

The smoke of the huts rises
among the maize : and that of the brick-kiln.
There is a factory a long way off, at the very
foot of the hills, whose smoke is far far higher.
            And on the bluish plateau
the long smoke of a train, and its long whistle.

The sound of cars accelerating,
and buses, down on the main road.
        And the tap tap of the stonebreaker
        hammering away at his stones.

On this side :   a heavy lorry
                    grinding up a hill . . .

Goats pass with tinkling bells,
leave lingering on the air
a gentle smell of goat
and goatsmilk.
            The birds are singing;
in Santa María de Ahuacatitlán
bells are ringing.

The setting sun gilds Teposteco
and tinges the snow on Popo pink.
            Cone
like strawberry ice-cream.

The moon comes up behind
Popocatépetl.

     *

(Moon pallid as a cloud,
and a cloud above Popo like snow
with Popo's snow the moon.)

     *

The lights of Cuernavaca twinkle in the distance :
those of Cuautla too, further, almost in the sky
tiny and bunched together, almost amongst the stars.
Somewhere in the fields a radio, playing a *corrido*.
A million crickets shrilling in the pastures.
            Each starts and stops and starts.
Do crickets never sleep?
                    Fireflies
flicker like stars, like Cuautla
like Cuernavaca.

     *

A train whistles in the distance,
deep in the night.
                Mournfully,
three times.
The old train to the capital,
like a lonely bird
calling its missing mate.

On Lake Nicaragua

Slow cargo-launch, midnight, mid-lake,
bound from San Miguelito to Granada.
The lights ahead not yet in sight,
the dwindling ones behind completely gone.
Only the stars
(the mast a finger pointing to the Seven Sisters)
           and the moon, rising above Chontales.

Another launch (just one red light) goes by
and sinks into the night.
We, for them :
           another red light sinking in the night ...
And I watching the stars, lying on the deck
between bunches of bananas and Chontales cheeses,
wonder : perhaps there's one that is an earth like ours
and someone watching me (watching the stars)
from another launch, on another night, on another lake.

Destruction of Santiago de Quauhtemalan

When news of the death of Pedro de Alvarado came,
Doña Beatriz gave orders that the entire palace
was to be painted black inside and out, halls, courtyards,
kitchens, corridors, stables, outhouses and latrines, even
the roofs,
          all painted black,
and hung with black curtains. This
because the Adelantado had died in Muchitiltic
(meaning "all black"), so named
since all the way from Muchitiltic to Iztlán
both earth and stones are equally and wholly black.
And the cathedral was draped with black hangings
and the whole city was in mourning
in memory of the Adelantado.
And Doña Beatriz stayed locked in a darkened room,
with blackened walls, not wanting to see the light,
neither the light of a window nor yet the light of a candle,
black-skirted and black-wimpled,
weeping and weeping, sighing, talking to herself
and crying out from time to time.
Nor would she eat nor drink nor sleep
nor yet consent to be consoled by any,
saying

> *that there remained no greater harm which God could do*
> > *to her than he had done already.*

She said :
> *What greater harm can God still have in store
> > since he has taken from me my good lord the Adelantado?*

And she said her name thereafter would be Doña Beatriz the Luckless.
The Council met in order to elect a Governor
and chose Doña Beatriz de la Cueva to be Governor.
The Councillors and Justices went formally
to the room in which Doña Beatriz had locked herself
and said that they had chosen her, naming her
Governor in the name of his Majesty the King of Spain.
And she accepted the charge and took the oath
upon the cross of the Governor's staff of office
signing the book of the Council :
> > *Doña Beatriz*
> > *The Luckless*

but then struck out her name in ink
with a great thick line, longer than the name,
so that all that should be legible should be :
> > ~~*Doña Beatriz*~~
> > *The Luckless*

And the skies of Guatemala clouded over
and filled with massive thunderheads
> > and lightning flashes and sheet-lightning

and it began to rain on Thursday the eighth day of September,
and it rained all that day,
> > and the next,
> > > and the next,

whilst the Volcán de Fuego spewed forth flames.
And on the Sunday, two hours after midnight,
the Volcán de Agua was seen crowned with lightnings

and then the first shock came with a roaring
as though a multitude of carriages careered below the ground
beneath the City of Guatemala; then came more tremors
and a greater roaring and the Volcán de Agua leapt
as though it wished to leave the earth, and the waters
of its crater-lake flowed down the side plunging and thrusting
bearing trees and rocks the size of caravels
and that river of earth and water and trees and rocks
raced towards the palace of Pedro de Alvarado the Adelantado
bearing with it the walls and roofs of houses,
coming out of windows
and pushing men out of windows,
whilst the Volcán de Fuego roared and rumbled
    and poured out rivers of fire.
   Sending out flashes and what looked like flaming
   comets.

And the water rose to the chamber of Doña Beatriz.
Who came out of the chamber wrapped in a coverlet
and summoned her maids, and ran with them into the oratory.

And the water kept on rising up the stonebuilt stairs
        reached
the first landing,
   crept upwards from step to step,
reached the second landing,
and reached the floor of the oratory.
Doña Beatriz took refuge on the altar with her maids,
embracing both an image of Christ crucified and
the small daughter of the Adelantado, while black water
rose above the first step of the altar,
and above the second,
      covered the altar,
reached their knees,
began to flow out of the windows;
    then the earth shook yet again

and the walls of the oratory fell in
on Doña Beatriz the Luckless and her maids.

And the river of stones and mud went from street to street
and district to district, knocking the houses down;
or sweeping them away with those inside
to strand the houses elsewhere in the city.

The night was very dark, faces could not be seen,
and the thunder continued,
           and the lightning continued,
and in the light of the flashes
           one could see great rocks
go floating down the streets like corks
entangled with bodies, furniture, doorways, and dead horses.

The wind made the trees groan
and the moaning and roaring of beasts could be heard
through the rushing of the waters, together
with the clatter of rolling rocks, the lowing
of cattle, the screams of women and children, from
street to street and district to district.
And some saw what looked like devils shrieking in the air
and a black cow with a single horn
in the palace doorway of Doña Beatriz the Luckless.

In her palace only her own room was left intact
but Doña Beatriz had left her room;
and when the people came they found the bed still warm.

There died Alonso Velasco and his wife and children
and no one was found in their house neither dead nor living,
indeed not even the foundations of the house itself remained.
Of the household of Martín Sánchez
no one was ever seen again.
There died Francisco Flores, the one-armed.
There died Blas Fernández, the blind.

There died Robles, the tailor, and his wife.
There died the wife of Francisco López,
and the wife of Alonso Martín, and their grand-daughters,
also the children of Juan Páez.

At dawn the Volcán de Agua was seen to lack its summit,
the city was deep in mud and filled with trees and rocks
and corpses. Squares, streets and districts could not be
   distinguished,
nor yet the site of houses.
                      A light rain was still falling.

The procession of the dead took place, with chanted litanies.
And the bishop bade them remove the mourning from the
   churches
and suspend the obsequies of the Adelantado.

                                  (an episode from *El estrecho dudoso*)

Managua 6.30 pm

The neon lights are gentle in the twilight
and the mercury lamps are pale and beautiful . . .
And the red star of a wireless mast
is as lovely as Venus
in Managua in the evening sky
and an Esso advertisement is like the moon

There is something mystical about the red tail-lights of cars

(The soul is like a girl kiss-smothered behind a car)
    TACA BUNGE KLM SINGER
    MENNEN HTM GOMEZ NORGE
    RPM SAF OPTICA SELECTA
proclaim the glory of God!
(Kiss me beneath the neon signs oh Lord)
    KODAK TROPICAL RADIO F & C REYES
spell out your Name
in many-coloured lights.
               "They bear
the good tidings . . ."
I recognize no other
meaning in them
I do not defend the cruelties behind these lights
And if I am to give a verdict on my age
it is this : Barbarous and primitive it was
but yet poetic

Unrighteous Mammon

In respect of riches, then, just or unjust,
of goods be they ill-gotten or well-gotten :
                    All riches are unjust.
All goods,
        ill-gotten.
If not by you, by others.
Your title-deeds may be in order. But
did you buy your land from its true owner?
And he from its true owner? And the latter ... ?
Though your title go back to the grant of a king
                            was
the land ever the king's?
Has no one ever been deprived of it?
And the money you receive legitimately now
from client or Bank or National Funds
                or from the US Treasury
was it ill-gotten at no point? Yet
do not think that in the perfect Communist State
Christ's parables will have lost relevance
or Luke 16. 9 have lost validity
                and riches be no longer UNJUST
or that you will no longer have a duty to distribute them.

Prayer for Marilyn Monroe

Lord accept this girl
called Marilyn Monroe throughout the world
though that was not her name
(but you know her real name, that of the orphan raped at nine
the shopgirl who tried to kill herself when aged sixteen)
who now goes into your presence without make-up
without her Press Agent
without her photographs or signing autographs
lonely as an astronaut facing the darkness of outer space.

When a girl, she dreamed she was naked in a church
        (according to *Time*)
standing in front of a prostrate multitude, heads to the ground,
and had to walk on tiptoe to avoid the heads.
You know our dreams better than all psychiatrists.
Church, house or cave all represent the safety of the womb
but also something more . . .
The heads are admirers, so much is clear (that
mass of heads in the darkness below the beam to the screen)
but the temple isn't the studios of 20th-Century Fox.
The temple, of marble and gold, is the temple of her body
in which the Son of Man stands whip in hand
driving out the money-changers of 20th-Century Fox
who made your house of prayer a den of thieves.

Lord, in this world
contaminated equally by radioactivity and sin,
surely you will not blame a shopgirl
who (like any other shopgirl) dreamed of being a star.
And her dream became "reality" (Technicolor reality).
All she did was follow the script we gave her,
that of our own lives, but it was meaningless
Forgive her, Lord, and likewise all of us
for this our 20th Century
and the Mammoth Super-Production in whose making we all
   shared.

She was hungry for love and we offered her tranquillizers.
For the sadness of our not being saints
       they recommended psychoanalysis.
Remember, Lord, her increasing terror of the camera
and hatred of make-up (yet insistence on being newly made-up
for every scene) and how the terror grew
and how her unpunctuality at the studios grew.

Like any other shopgirl she dreamed
of being a star.
And her life was as unreal as a dream an analyst reads and files.

Her romances were kisses with closed eyes
which when the eyes are opened
are seen to have been played out beneath the spotlights
       but the spotlights have gone out,
and the two walls of the room (it was a set) are taken down
while the Director moves away notebook in hand,
       the scene being safely canned.
Or like a cruise on a yacht, a kiss in Singapore, a dance in Rio;
a reception in the mansion of the Duke and Duchess of Windsor
       viewed in the sad tawdriness of a cheap apartment.

The film ended without the final kiss.
They found her dead in bed, hand on the phone

And the detectives knew not whom she was about to call.
It was as
though someone had dialled the only friendly voice
and heard a pre-recorded tape just saying "WRONG NUMBER";
or like someone wounded by gangsters, who
reaches out towards a disconnected phone.

Lord, whomsoever
it may have been that she was going to call
but did not (and perhaps it was no one at all
or Someone not named in the Los Angeles directory),
      Lord, answer that phone.

Blessed is the man

Blessed is the man that heeds not the dictates of the Party,
nor attends any of its meetings;
nor sits down at table with the gangsters
nor yet with Generals in courts-martial.
Blessed is the man that spies not on his brother
nor betrays him with whom he went to school.
Blessed is the man that reads not advertisements,
nor pays heed unto broadcasts,
nor yet gives credence unto slogans.

    For he shall be like a tree, planted by the rivers of water.

Why hast thou forsaken me?

My God, my God, oh why hast thou forsaken me?
I am but the travesty of a man
    despised of the people,
laughed unto scorn in every daily paper.
Their armoured cars encompass me,
their machine-gunners have set their sights on me,
barbed wire besets me round.
From morning until evening
I must answer to my name;
they have tattooed me with a number.
They have photographed me
    hedged about by an electric fence.
My bones may all be told as on an X-ray screen.
They have taken my identity away from me.
They have led me naked to the gas-chamber;
and they have parted my garments among them—
    yea, even down to my shoes.
I call out for morphia but no one hears;
I call out in the strait-jacket,
call out all night long in lunatic asylums—
in the ward for terminal cases,
in the isolation wing,
in the home for the aged.

Drenched in sweat, I suffer
in the psychiatric clinic, stifle
in the oxygen-tent, and weep
in the police station,
     in the prison yard,
          in the torture chamber,
              in the orphanage;
I am contaminated by radioactivity
     and all men shun me lest it might smite them.

But my words shall be of thee before my brethren,
and I shall exalt thee before the congregation of our people;
my hymns shall rise up in the midst of a multitude.
There will be a banquet set before those that are poor.
And there shall be a great feast among our people :
the new people, that is to be born.

Thou art our ally Lord

Lord declare war on those that war on us
because thou art our ally

Great are the powers arrayed against us
but the weapons of the Lord are yet more fearful

We attacked them not and yet they persecute us
we did not conspire against them yet we are imprisoned

        Gangsters have set snares for me

Lord
     Thou wilt deliver us from the dictator
from the exploiters of the proletariat and the poor
False witnesses rose up against me
to question me on matters which I knew not of
The interrogators confront me
and place a confession of conspiracy before me
a confession of espionage and sabotage

By their own political systems shall they be brought low
and they shall be purged even as they did purge

Their propaganda scoffs at us
        deriding us

How long oh Lord how long wilt thou stay neutral
a spectator merely looking on?

Deliver me from the torture-chamber
free me from the concentration camp
Their propaganda never speaks of peace
                      They seek to provoke war
Hearing their radio
                      and watching their TV
keep thou no longer silent!

Awake
      take up my cause
                    oh God
                              come to my aid!

Let them not say
                "We have made an end of our political
                      opponents"
Cast them into confusion, put them to shame
they that announce our destruction in press-conferences
and announce it with rejoicing
Rather let those who are for us rejoice

I shall praise thee in my poems
                all the days of my life

Their shares shall wither as the grass

Fret not that they make many millions
For their stocks and shares
                          are as the grass of the fields
Neither be envious of millionaires or film-stars
or of those who get a full eight-column spread
or those who live in luxury hotels
lunching in luxurious restaurants
for soon their names will not appear in any newspaper
nor will even the learned know their names
        For they shall soon be cut down like the grass of the fields

Fret not at their inventions
                          nor at their technology
A little while, and the Leader you see you will not see
you will seek him in his palace
                          and not find him
Leadership will pass unto the meek
                          (the "pacifists")

They enlarge the concentration camps
invent new kinds of torture
new methods of "investigation"
They rest not in the night for making plans
plans how to overcome us
                          and exploit us more

but the Lord laughs at them
knowing they will shortly fall from power
The arms they manufacture will turn against them
Their political systems will be swept from the face of the earth
their political parties will no longer exist
And their technicians' plans will come to naught

The great powers
                    are as the flowers of the field
All empires
        but as smoke

They spy upon us all the day
The sentences which they will pass on us are prearranged
But the Lord will not deliver us to their police
nor let us be condemned when brought to trial
I have seen the dictator's portrait everywhere
                        —it spread like a flourishing tree—
and then I passed that way again
                              it was not there
I sought it and I found it not
I sought it and I found no portrait
nor might his name be named

Hear this all you peoples

Hear this all you peoples
        Give ear all you inhabitants of the earth
you plebeians and nobility
you proletarians and millionaires
                      all classes of society
My mouth shall speak in proverbs
        and of wisdom
                with an harp . . .
            "Wherefore should I fear persecution
            from those who put their trust in Banks
            and expectations in Insurance Policies?"

Life cannot be bought with a cheque
its shares stand very high
they cannot be paid for with money

To live forever and not see the tomb :
nobody can buy that policy

They thought that they would live forever
        and would forever stay in power
and they gave their names to their lands
to all the properties they stole
they took the names away from cities
renaming them after themselves

Their statues stood in every square
            yet who recalls them now?
Their bronze statues were pulled down
bronze plaques ripped out of walls
Their palace is now a mausoleum
So do not fret when you see one grow rich
or owning many millions
or if the glory of his house increases
or he becomes renowned as a strong man
For in death he shall have no dominion
no party at his call
Though while he lived the official press proclaimed:
"You shall be praised because felicity is yours!"
yet shall he go to the dwelling of his fathers
           and see the light no more

But the man set high in office does not understand
The man that is in power
The ruler both bemedalled and well-fed
He laughs believing he will never die
not knowing he is like the animals
doomed to be slain on the day of rejoicing

Apocalypse

    AND BEHOLD
    I saw an angel
               (all his cells were electronic eyes)
and heard a supersonic voice
saying : Open up your typewriter and type
        and I beheld a silver projectile in flight
    which went from Europe to America in twenty minutes
whose name was the H-Bomb
               (and hell flew with it)
    I saw a flying saucer fall from heaven
The seismographs plotted a shock like to an earthquake
and all the artificial planets fell to earth
        the President of the National Radiation Council
        the Director of the Atomic Energy Commission
        the Secretary of State for Defence
              were deep in sheltering caves
And the first angel set off the warning siren
    and there followed hail and fire : Strontium 90 rained
    from the heavens
                   Caesium 137
                   Carbon 14
And the second angel set off the warning siren
and all eardrums were shattered for 300 miles
by the sound of the explosion
all retinas which saw the flash of the explosion
were seared throughout those same 300 miles

                    the heat at ground zero was like that of the sun
           and steel and iron and glass and concrete were burnt up
                        and sucked into the skies to fall as radioactive rain
           and there was loosed a hurricane wind the force of Hurricane
              Flora
           and three million cars and trucks flew up into the skies
           crashed into buildings
                                burst like Molotov cocktails
           And the third angel set off the warning siren
           and I beheld a mushroom-cloud above New York
                                and a mushroom-cloud above Moscow
                   and a mushroom-cloud above London
                                     and a mushroom-cloud above
                                       Peking
           (Hiroshima's fate was become the subject of envy)
           And all stores and all museums and all libraries
           and all the beauties of the earth
                                    were now burnt up
           and raised to form the cloud of radioactive dust
           which hung about the planet poisoning it
                the radioactive rain gave leukaemia unto some
                                    lung-cancer unto others
                     and unto others cancer of the bone
                                           or cancer of the
                                               ovaries
           children were born with cataract
           and the genes of man suffered unto the twenty-second generation.
                             And this was known as the Forty-five-
                                  minute War . . .
              Seven angels came
           bearing cups of smoke in their hands
                         (smoke like a mushroom-cloud)
           and first I saw the great cup raised over Hiroshima
                              (like a cornet of venomous ice-cream)
                      engendering one vast malignant ulcer

and the cup of the second was poured into the sea
    making the whole sea radioactive
                              so that all fish died
and the third angel poured forth a neutronic cup
which seared men with a fire like solar fire
and the fourth angel poured his cup which was of Cobalt
and it was given unto Babylon to drain the chalice of the grapes
   of wrath
And the loud voice cried :
    Smite her with twice the megatons with which she smote !
And the angel who controlled the firing of this bomb
                          pushed down the firing key
And they said unto me : You have as yet not seen the Typhus
   bomb
                    nor yet Q fever
I continued watching the vision in the night
and in my vision I beheld as on TV
emerging from the masses
                a Machine
    fearful and terrible beyond all measure
and like a bear or an eagle or a lion with the wings of aircraft
many propellers numerous antennae eyes of radar
its brain a computer programmed to give the Number of the
   Beast
roaring its orders unto men
                         through hosts of microphones
and all men went in fear of the Machine
Likewise I saw the aircraft in my vision
aircraft faster than sound bearing 50-megaton bombs
and no man guided them but the Machine alone
they flew to every city of the earth
each one precisely on target
And the angel said : Can you discern Columbus Circle now?
      Or the place where the United Nations Building
         stood?

And where Columbus Circle was
              I saw but a hole in which a 50-storey block
            might fit
and where the United Nations Building stood
I saw but a great grey cliff moss-grown and duck-bespattered
with wave-swept rocks beyond it seagulls crying
And in the heavens I beheld a mighty light
            like a million-megaton explosion
and I heard a voice saying unto me : Switch on your radio
and I did switch it on and heard : BABYLON IS FALLEN
                  BABYLON THE GREAT IS FALLEN
and all transmitters in the world gave the same news
And the angel gave me a cheque drawn on the National City
  Bank
and said unto me : Go cash this cheque
but no bank would for they had all closed down
Skyscrapers were as though they had never been
A million simultaneous fires yet not one firefighter
nor a phone to summon an ambulance nor were there ambulances
nor was there enough plasma in the world
                      to help the injured of a single
                      city
And I heard another voice from heaven saying :
                  Go forth from her my people
Lest you be contaminated by the radiation
            lest you be smitten by the microbes
    by the Anthrax Bomb
            by the Cholera Bomb
      by the Diphtheria Bomb
              by the Tularaemia Bomb
They will behold the magnitude of the disaster on TV
        for the bomb is fallen on great Babylon
weeping and wailing for the city that they loved
pilots will look down from planes and draw not nigh
the ocean liners will cast anchor far away

for fear lest the atomic leprosy should fall on them
On every waveband there was a voice heard saying :
>> ALLELUIA

And the angel carried me away in the spirit into the wilderness
>> and the wilderness blossomed with
>> laboratories

and there the Devil enacted his atomic tests
And I beheld the Great Whore riding on the Beast
(the Beast was a technological Beast slogan-bedecked)
and the whore came clutching all manner of stocks and shares
and bonds
and of commercial documents
her harlot's voice sang drunkenly as in a night-club
in her left hand she bore a cup of blood
for she was drunk with the blood of all those tortured
all those purged all those condemned by military courts
all those sent to the wall
and of whomsoever had resisted upon earth
>> with the martyrs of
>> Jesus

and she smiled with golden teeth
>> the lipstick on her mouth being
>> blood

and the angel said unto me : The heads which you saw on the
Beast
are dictators, and the horns which you saw are revolutionary
leaders
who are not dictators yet but will be when they have gained
power
and these shall make war with the Lamb
>> and the Lamb shall
>> overcome them

And he said unto me : the nations of the world are divided
>> into two blocks (Gog and Magog)

yet the two blocks are in truth but the one

(which is against the Lamb)
                        and fire will fall from heaven to consume them
                    both
And in the earth's biology I saw a New Evolution
as though a New Planet had appeared in space
For death and hell were passed away in nuclear fire
and neither were there peoples as before
but I saw rather a new species freshly evolved
a species not made up of individuals
but rather one sole organism
                              made up of men in place of cells
and all biologists were mightily amazed
But men were free and in their union were one Person—
                            not a Machine—
and the sociologists were equally astounded
Such men as had no part in this new species
                            were but as fossils
The Organism enclosed the whole curve of the planet
round as a cell (but planetary in dimensions)
and the Cell was garlanded as a Bride awaiting the Bridegroom
and the Earth rejoiced
          (as the Earth had rejoiced when the first cell divided)
And there was a New Canticle
and all other inhabited planets heard the earth
          singing that song of love

Quetzal feathers dry—in time

Quetzal feathers dry, in time,
mosaics of hummingbird's feathers fade like flowers
mosaics of turquoise, jade, obsidian, mother-of-pearl
fall like flowers.
Necklaces of shells or jade are scattered
                    like strings of cacao blossom . . .

Vessels white as leaves of codices
      with figures in dark red and in light red
   in yellow
              turquoise-green
red earthen vessels the colour of red chilli
and the red earthen pots from Oaxaca like ripe fruit
or orange-hued like flame
                    grow dim or shatter.
    A temple pyramid
will crumble.
Quetzal feathers grow dim
              and gather dust!
I, King Netzahualcóyotl, lament : pay heed!
The universe is as a game in the ball-court.
A game played with two balls : the Sun and the Moon.
Against the powers of hell.
We know not who will win (the loser dies).

Look how the Sun stands at the centre of the Calendar—
    the symbol of the Sun is at the very centre—
Tonatiuh in the morning ("rising eagle")
being like an eagle flying upwards in the morning
to a *nopal* to crush men's hearts like cactus-fruit;
Cuauhtémoc in the evening
              ("sinking eagle").
The rubber ball goes up and down, and comes and goes,
and men must play with it.
Life and death : the black ink and the red,
the twin hues poets use to paint their codices.

The lake of Texcoco and Tenochtitlán
           ("lake of the moon")
which is like an obsidian mirror in the moonlight
and by the light of the sun the quiet blue-green
         of tranquil turquoise
    emerald and golden
lake of flowery waters—where the duck swims
and swimming comes and goes
calls out in flight moving its sun-filled tail—
will in the end dry out as flowers dry.

The lake of Texcoco and Tenochtitlán
           ("lake of the moon")
will be like a dream we dreamt on a moonlight night.
Which vanishes with daylight, dries.
        Dust swirling where it stood.

It is because of this my song is sad
and has the sad accompaniment of the *teponaztli*.
Ask not why the *teponaztli* has so sad a sound!

We are only here on earth to dream
to leave a few illuminated manuscripts
                      like dreams.
The pottery of the Toltecs lies beneath the ground
scattered like the petals of flowers.

We have painted the heart of heaven upon deerskin
but will those who come after comprehend the Codex?

Our poems on paper made from maguey, yucca or palm
will be carried away by the wind as the dust of Texcoco.

Those who knew the court of ancient Tezozómoc
tyrant king—
with dancers clad as jaguars or birds
huehuetl players crowned with flowers
and gardens sounding with the timbrels of their fountains—
would only find a heap of stones today
where owls sing death.
He who bore down on the humble and the weak, the *macehuales*
who cut and carry wood or seek maguey :
the *macehual* now gathers his maguey and wood
amongst the remants of great Tezozómoc's baths.

The reigns of kings are brief as roses.
Those princes dressed in quetzal feathers
princesses with obsidian eyes
where are they now?
Go seek them in royal funerary jars
             and find these full of dust.
Gone like Popocatépetl's smoke . . .
Mere shades in Mictlan, Region of Mystery.
        Be not surprised the *teponaztli*
            has so sad a sound.
                       I Netzahualcóyotl
will soon be in my earthen jar mingled with earth
(a mere few bones with necklaces)
made of earth like any earthen vessel
    like any earthen vessel back to earth
the King of Texcoco will be no different from any *macehual*.

But watch the Sun rise daily from the Region of the dead, from
  Mictlan,

or Quetzalcóatl the star which dies to be reborn—
how bright rides Quetzalcóatl as Morning Star!
Watch the maize and how it dies to rise
all young and tender after the first rains which Tláloc sends.
If there is nothing in the jar save dust
know I am being ground like maize by Mother Cihuacóatl
and that my bones will live and flower again!
Quetzalcóatl will bring me back from Mictlan.
No one can change this Codex, in the black ink and the red,
whose pictures sing the praises of Him through whom all live
    Lord of the near and Lord of inwardness.

(Cantares Mexicanos, I)

Economy of Tahuantinsuyu

They had no money
     gold was for making lizards
     and NOT COINS
         garments
              which flashed like flame
        in the light of the sun or of bonfires
the images of the gods
        and of the women they loved
but not coins
   Thousands of forges shining in the Andean night
and with their abundance of gold and silver
        they had no money
they knew
     how to cast laminate solder engrave
the gold and the silver
   gold : the sweat of the sun
        silver : the tears of the moon
     Threads beads filigree
          brooches
          pectorals
          rattles
  but not MONEY
    and because there was no money

                        there was neither prostitution nor theft
                the doors of the houses were left open
nor government corruption nor embezzlement
                        every 2 years they
                                rendered account of their deeds in Cuzco
because there was neither commerce nor money
                                                there was no
selling of Indians
                No Indian was ever sold
And there was chicha for all

They knew not the inflationary value of money
their coin was the Sun which shines for all alike
belongs to all and which makes all things grow
the Sun which knows neither inflation nor deflation :
And not those soiled Peruvian *soles* (= "suns") a *peón* gets
(for one such *sol* he will show you his ruins)
All ate 2 meals a day throughout the Empire

                        And it was not financiers
                        who created Inca myths

Later all the gold was looted from the temples of the Sun
and set to circulate in ingots
                        stamped with Pizarro's initials
Coinage brought taxation and in the time
of the Colony the first beggars appeared

The water no longer sings in the stone channels
the roads are broken
the lands as dry as mummies
                        as the mummies
of happy girls who danced
in *Airiway* (April)
                the Month of the Dance of the New Maize
now dry and crouching on their hunkers in museums

Manco Capac! Manco Capac!
                                    Rich in virtues not in money
(Mancjo : "virtue", Capacj : "rich")
"Man rich in Virtues"
An economic system without COINAGE
the moneyless society of which we dream
They valued gold but it was
in the same way as they valued rose quartz or grass
and they offered it to eat
                    as grass
         to the horses of the conquistadors
upon seeing them chew metal (champ the bit)
                        with foam-flecked mouths
They had no money
and no one died of hunger in all the Empire
and the hue of their ponchos has lasted a thousand years
even princesses span
the blind were employed in husking maize
the children in hunting birds
KEEP THE INDIANS OCCUPIED
                          was an Inca slogan
the lame the maimed the old all worked
         none was idle nor was unemployed
and food was given to all those who could not work
the Inca himself worked painting and drawing
When the Empire fell
                the Indian settled down on his hunkers
like a heap of ashes
and since that time has done no more than think ...
         indifferent to skyscrapers
     to the Alliance for Progress
               Think? Who knows?
The builder of Macchu Picchu
in his house of old cans
                    and Quaker Oat cartons

The emerald-cutter stinking and starving
               (the tourist snaps him)
As alone as a cactus
and silent as the Andean landscape in the background
                            Nothing but ashes
      but ashes
stirred by the breeze off the Andes
The sad-faced llama wood-laden
stares mutely at the tourist
close by its owners

They had no money
                     No one was ever sold
Nor were the miners exploited
FORBIDDEN
to mine the mercury which moves like snakes
             (because it caused trembling in the Indians)
Forbidden to fish for pearls
And the army was not hated by the people
The function of the State
                        was to feed the people
The land belonged to the tiller
         and not to the *latifundista*
And the Seven Sisters guarded the maize-plots
         There was land enough for all
               Water and guano free
(there was no monopoly in guano)
Mandatory banquets for the people
And when the agricultural year began
the land was divided up with singing and chicha
      to the sound of the drum of tapir hide
      to the sound of the flute of jaguar bone
the Inca ploughed the first furrow with a plough of gold
Even the mummies had their pouch of grain
for the journey beyond

Domestic animals were protected
there was legislation for llamas and vicuñas
even the beasts of the jungle had a code
          (which the Children of the Sun do not today)

From the Square of Happiness in Cuzco
        (which was the centre of the world)
           ran the 4 highways
to the 4 regions into which the Empire was divided
     "The Four Horizons"
  TAHUANTINSUYU
         And the hanging bridges
over raging rivers
           paved roads
tracks snaking across the hills
all came together
     in the Square of Happiness in Cuzco
       the centre of the world

The heir to the throne
     succeeded his father on the throne
         BUT DID NOT INHERIT HIS POSSESSIONS
An agrarian communism?
Yes, an agrarian communism
    THE SOCIALIST EMPIRE OF THE INCAS
Neruda : freedom did not exist
               but there was social security
And not everything was perfect in the "Inca Paradise"
The knotted *quipu* of history was censored
Free motels on the highways
     but no freedom to travel
And what of Atahualpa's purges?
            The scream of the exile
in the Amazonian jungle?
           The Inca was god
              was Stalin

                    (There could be no Opposition)
The bards sang only the official history
Amaru Tupac was erased from the roll of kings

But their myths
                    were not created by financiers!
Religious truth
                    and political truth
were but the one truth for the people
An economy which *did have* religion
                    the Inca's lands were the last to be tilled
first those of the Sun (those of religion)
then those of widows and orphans
then those of the people
                    and the lands of the Inca the last to be tilled

An Empire of *ayllus*
                    ayllus of working families
even beasts plants ores
                    grouped into *ayllus*
the entire universe one great *Ayllu*
(today, instead of the *ayllu* : *latifundios*)
The land could not be bartered
Llacta mama (the earth) belonged to all
                    was Mother of all

The harvest was a time for joyful song and chicha
today panic on the Stock Exchange at a good harvest
            —the Spectre of Abundance—
AP. NEW YORK
                    (on that long strip of yellow paper)
WORLD SUGAR FUTURES SLUMPED TODAY
SALES HIT BY DROP IN EXPORT PRICES
AND PREDICTIONS OF WORLD RECORD HARVEST
just as the Stock Exchange shudders
                    at the Bogey of Peace
the teletype trembles

THE STOCK MARKET TODAY EXPERIENCED ITS SHARPEST FALL
US STEEL 3.1 TO 322.5, BASE METALS 0.42 TO 70.98 MC1038AES
                    (on that long yellow strip)
Now
earthenware is drab and sad
the carmine of *achiote*
                    no longer smiles on textiles
weaving is poor
             its style has coarsened
     fewer threads per inch
             and they no longer spin the "perfect thread"
Llacta mama (the earth) belongs to the landowners
the golden butterfly lies imprisoned in the Bank
the dictator is rich in money not in virtues
             and oh how sad
                 how sad the music of the *yaravies*
The Inca Empire now confined
             to the unreal domains of coca-leaf
                                       or chicha
       (then only are they free and gay
                 and raise their voices
recapturing the Inca Empire)

On the *puna*
             one sad flute
                                one
note as delicate as moonlight
             and the plaint of a *quena*
with a Quecchua song...
                    Chaupi punchapi tutayaca
                             ("darkness at noon")
       a herdsman passes with a flock of llamas
and the bells tinkle
         among huge slabs of rock
                       which once had been
             a burnished wall

Will Manco Capac with his plough of gold one day come back?
And will the Indian speak once more?
Can one ever
                reconstitute the glowing vessel
                        from these sherds?
Reassemble
        the monoliths
                  into a massive wall
so neatly that a knife-blade will not slide between them?
that a knife-blade will not slide between them ...
Restore the broken roads
    of South America
right to the Four Horizons
                  for swift communication as of old?
And will the Indian's universe become a great *Ayllu* once again?

The journey was to the Beyond and not to the museum
    in which today behind the glass
the mummy's withered hand still clings
        to its pouch of grain.

Katun 11 Ahau

Katun of dishonourable governors and many arrows,
of sadness in the huts,
                               and whispering,
    and vigilance by night.
In this *katun* we weep
for the books that were burnt,
the exiles from the kingdom. And the loss
of maize
and loss of cosmic knowledge.

Greed pestilence rocks skulls.

Lord Mountain Cat. Lord Honey Bear. The jaguar of the people.
In this *katun* the *chilan* writes :
                      "people eat stones
                      eat sticks".
The *katun* in which great tributes are collected,
    in which the mask is stolen,
in which the treasure buried in the *milpa* is stolen.
In this *katun* invaders never lack;
                the enemies of the land.
Suckers of blood ! . . .
                Gnats battening on the peoples.
The emptiers of the great earthen jars.
Our life like badgers, in the jungle, is hard.
They scorn our knowledge of the universe :
a book in which we read for people's good.
    (In this *katun* we are derided for our dress.)

               The hieroglyphs are lost beneath the thickets.
Our civilization with black vultures overhead.
Our dwellings flattened by the hurricane.
The nobles now *peones* mending roads.
The people bowed beneath a mountain in a net.
And governments : are like the drought...
And we say : would that there might return
          he who first built an arch,
     wrote prayers,
devised the calendar permitting chronicles and histories
           and auguries of things to come.
Now however, in the meanwhile, like the badger.
Saddest of moons,
saddest of moons in the sky of the Petén.
Oppression...
              And vigilance in the night.
Our lord the Honey Bear is lecherous...

The *chilan* ("he that is mouth") writes thus :
            "The Plague is great, and great the Hurricane"
    In the blue sea the pointed fin
    the pointed fin
             of evil-minded Xooc, man-eating shark.

But the *katun* of the Cruel Men will pass.
The Katun of the Tree of Life shall be established.
And a benevolent rule.
The people be no longer bidden to eat less.
The Katun Union-for-a-Common-Cause,
the Katun of "Good Living Conditions"...
No longer shall we have to keep our voices low.
The *chilan* says the people will be a united people.
Many will come together to sing together.
        And then there will be no more Honey Bear.
The stone beneath the thickets will again display

its noble face. The square stone
>   wear a countenance.

The governors will be good, to the people's joy.
>   The lords : legitimate.
Abundance in the mountains, and fair rituals.

It is the time for building the new pyramid
>   upon the basis of the old.

The evil-minded Xooc, the Shark, has been harpooned.
And the people will never lack for a *chilan*.
The Chilan :
>   he who reads the sacred scriptures
and studies the skies by night.
—The movements of the Sun and of the Moon
in order that the time to till the land be known,
the time to harvest maize,
>   to burn the fields,
>   to set the traps,
to search the woods for deer.
The Chilan : he sets the days for rain.
The days when men shall sing.
The ending of the rainy season.
Wards off both plagues and hunger.
Distributes food should hunger come.
Invigilates the carving of the stelae,
>   designs new temples,
delivers tablets which predict eclipses.

Night

        The dark night of the soul (or Nothing!)
        Night without moon or sometimes moonlit.
        In the interior emptiness, company.
        An emptiness of all to possess ALL.
        The dark night of kisses : light
        is seen as a mist in this night.
        In dream and forgetfulness, knowing not how.
        The flavour of love unknowing uncomprehending.
        Night. The supper that rests and that enamours.

And you, what do you want? Shares in Du Pont?
To go to bed with Miss Sweden or Miss Brazil?

Fiery Ford 66 : luxurious comfort
Ford Galaxy 500/XL flame-coloured
city lights in the night in the background
and He and She reclining languorous inside
      He in tuxedo She with an orchid
(impressively new lines ... daring and elegant
      VISIT YOUR FORD AGENT)
or the yellow Pontiac in green pastures
      with an eternal picnic spread by its side
and She on the deck of a yacht in a check shirt
      dark glasses and a smile full of sunshine
hair gently wind-lifted and the sea blue-green
But do you know She doesn't exist? She doesn't exist.
Publicity
      is a painted whore!

Or the Pan American Jet Clipper white as snow
        floating in blue blue sky
Royal castle (Kodachrome) in the Bavarian Alps
or palm-trees in the foreground and a Tahiti beach
        the place of your dreams to which
        you never thought to go?
        CONSULT YOUR TRAVEL AGENT
or a walk along a Californian shore
He and She happy beside the sea
and carrying the picnic-basket between them.
A painted whore! No, She doesn't exist!

Shares in Du Pont? or a Du Pont directorship?
your house with fourteen gardens and Du Pont fungicide
    a twenty-room apartment full of antiques
        (a Georgian mansion?)
Vacations in Honolulu. The Riviera.
Hobbies: salmon-fishing in Scotland
        safaris in Africa
cups won by horse or hound.
Your Du Pont invented Nylon
and before that Cellophane
but earlier still he "made it" by selling munitions
(40% of the explosives used by the Allies in World War I)
Supersonic planes flying overhead all of the time
bomb-laden
        machines talking to other machines
    kennels with air-conditioning
the President assassinated on your TV screen
        babes burned with napalm.
And faces tense on the subway, tense
with terror in the offices
the daily terror on the radio
        and television.
A bomb in Algeria

Sometimes in the night, in the depth of our souls,
although we'd not admit it, we've seen Dracula.
      "Incompatibility of character"
  incompatibility for love
and advertisements singing the praises of woman.
And the turning and turning in our sleep each night
Those supersonic planes
      flying great circles in the night sky Superman
the bombs are not intended to be used they say

And you buy the product you are meant to buy
and think the thoughts which you are meant to think
dutifully answer all the questionnaires
and heed what the records say
the radio voice which gives you orders.
Shall we rebel? Shall
we smash windows?
              Throw bricks at shop-fronts?
And would that make us free?
              Would the Revolution make us free
like juvenile delinquents in stolen cars
careering down roads between commercial hoardings?
(They believe every advertisement they see, believe
           in trade-names and adore new cars)

Better to be beat saints
      zen cool jazz beards and sandals
always thumbing a lift to some New City
with no firm creed on which to lay their heads
the gatherers of trash and shovellers of snow—
      Voluntary Poverty.
Poor at the heart of prosperity.
Begging for alms on Isurgentes Avenue with a guitar
or selling a pint of blood to buy a meal
      they read not papers neither do they view TV
nor do they join political parties

Herod and the little foxes have their lairs
but there is nowhere for the Son of Man to lay his head.
They dropped out of civilization. Yet there's
still fear in their eyes. (The air
of someone, in a station, who jumped out
of an express train to an unknown destination).

But their trappings
are really more of a question
                              a question to others
than an answer
And the visions of lysergic acid
                are not the Vision
but
fantastic neon visions—
                       from the chemist's shop—
   Or like the invention of yet another plastic.
Visions sold by gangsters or else sold by Du Pont.
And they are so lonely, so un-united in their night
the night of an expanding universe
like he who puts an advertisement into the papers
     "desires correspondence with a young lady 18 to 23
        Box Number..."
Or: "desires correspondence with a gentleman..."
Or someone asking a computer for a pen-friend
speaking the same language and sharing the same tastes.

And if they have thought they kissed the Infinite
their kisses were lit by General Electric's fluorescent light.

Sor Josefa del Castillo y Guevara: seeker of Nothingness.
Or as Fernando González said to Gonzalo Arango:
Take up thy Cross.
And:
     "If they renounce the world, their world,
                but achieve not detachment from it..."

The dark night of the soul, or NOTHING.
And as it were being in the dark with nothing.
Dark night of kisses. The Lover and the Belovèd.
Light as a darkness in this night. And Nothing.
The silent music is not played on nylon strings.

Tahirassawichi in Washington

In 1898 Tahirassawichi went to Washington
"only to talk about religion"
                (as he said to the American government)
     only so that the old forms of prayer might be preserved.
He was wholly unimpressed by the Capitol.
The Library of Congress was all very well
but would be of no use to keep the sacred things
since these must be kept in a mud hut
          (although his own was tumbling down).
When asked whether he would use the elevator to ascend
the Washington Monument, or the stairs,
he answered : "I shall not go up. The white man
places stone upon stone to climb them. I shall not go up.
       I have climbed the hills which Tirawahat made."
And Tahirassawichi said to the State Department :
"The blue dome of the sky is Tirawahat's Lodge
              (we do not like clouds between him and
                  ourselves).
The first thing one must do
is choose a holy place in which to live
a place sacred to Tirawahat, where a man
may dwell in silence and in meditation.
Our round lodge is the nest (the nest
        where we dwell together and raise children).

At its heart the hearth binding us into a single family.
The door is for all persons to come in
and visions likewise come in by the door.
Blue is the colour of Tirawahat's Lodge
and we mix blue earth with river water
because the river stands for life, flowing
ceaselessly from generation unto generation.
The pot that is painted blue is the dome of the sky
and we paint a head of maize, the power of the earth.
But this power comes from above, from Tirawahat,
which is why we paint the head of maize his colour.
We offer tobacco smoke to Tirawahat :
        smoking was prayer before, not done for pleasure
        the White Man taught us to profane tobacco.
On the trail we greet all that we meet with song
for Tirawahat is in everything. We greet the rivers :
seen from a distance rivers are rows of trees
        and we sing to those trees
closer we see the line of water, and hear it ripple
and we sing to the water rippling on its way.
And we sing to the buffalo, not in prairies now
we sing the Song of the Buffalo in the lodge
for there are no longer any buffaloes.
And we sing the hills which Tirawahat made.
We climb them alone, and only when we go to pray.
Thence one sees if there are enemies. Or whether friends come.
It is because the hills are good for man that we sing them.
And we sing the mesetas, but these we sing in the lodge
for we ourselves have never seen mesetas
        those flat-topped hills, but
we are told that our forefathers often saw them
and we recall what they saw in the days of their journeying.
And we sing the dawn when it rises in the East
and all life is renewed

(this is a great mystery : I speak to you
        of something which is very sacred).
We sing the morning star
the morning star is like a man and painted red
        the colour of life.
We sing when the animals wake up
and come out of their hiding places.
The earliest is the deer followed by her fawn.
We sing when the sun strikes through the entrance of the lodge
and when it reaches the smokehole in the centre of the lodge
and at evening when there is no sunlight in the lodge
and the sun is on the hills which are like the walls
of one great lodge in which all peoples live.
We sing in the night-time, which is when dreams come.
For visions come more readily by night.
It is easier for them to travel over sleeping earth.
They near the lodge and halt at the lodge door
then enter the lodge, and fill it.
Were it not true dreams come
we should long have given up the songs.
And we sing at night when the Seven Sisters rise.
Seven stars always together
which help whoever is lost far from his village
(and teach mankind to live together as they do).
Tirawahat is father of all our dreams
and he perpetuates the tribe in our sons.
With blue water we paint Tirawahat's sign
(an arch with a straight line down the middle)
on a boy's face
        The arch goes on the forehead and the cheeks
        the straight line down the nose
(the arch is the blue vault of the sky where Tirawahat lives
and the line is his breath which comes down giving life.)
The boy's face represents the new generation
and the river water is the passing of the generations

and the blue earth that we miss is the sky of Tirawahat
(and the blue drawing that we sketch is Tirawahat's face).
Then we make the boy look into river water
and seeing the water he sees his own image
as though seeing in his own face his sons and the sons of his sons
but he also sees the blue face of Tirawahat
imaged in his own face and in the generations still to come.
Our lodge as I said has the shape of a nest
and if you go up onto a mountain and look all round
you will see the sky encloses the whole earth
and that the earth is round in the shape of a nest
so that all tribes may live together in union.
The storm may cast the eagle's nest down to the ground
but the nest of the oriole sways in the wind
        and stays unharmed."

Tahirassawichi, I suppose, has said nothing at all
        as far as the State Department is concerned.

In the half-light

In the half-light
    (the invitation being clandestine)
smiling girls move from table to table
with olives and sardines
    Irene serves the wine
there aren't a lot of us
    one cup for all mouths present
one great loaf
    for all
        one song on every lip.
    One song, and the one cup.
We men exchange a kiss of peace, the women kiss
There is a slave among us, there's Erastus
(city treasurer) the ex-rabbi Crispus
    and Titius Junius multimillionaire.
Grains of wheat scattered in the fields
        joined in a single loaf.
Scattered at pump or barracks or shop
    we meet on Saturdays, at twilight :
separate grapes joined in a single wine.
        Irene moves among the tables
and we talk together, recumbent,
until midnight, beneath the orange torches
What, until midnight? Until Sunday dawns.

There is one whom we see not, he who presides
    He who was put to death, crowned with vine-shoots,

round whom we dine, this being
      a funeral feast. He
celebrated thus before he died, that we
      might be thus drawn together afterwards
("do this in memory of me")
      and in this wine he lives.
Dawn comes. The lights grow pale.
      "Good-bye, Irene"
and in the misty streets we scatter
      yet remain united.

Death of Thomas Merton

Manrique said our lives were rivers
going down to the sea which is death
but the death they flow down to is life
And your death was more of a quirk, Merton
               (absurd as a zen koan?)
"Made by General Electric"
and your body flown to the States in an Army plane
     you'd have had a good laugh, given your sense of humour
you Merton bodiless and dying of laughter
likewise myself
The initiates of Dionysus used ivy leaves . . .
       I knew it not:
I tap out this word "death" with joy today
Dying isn't something like a car-smash
                 or a short-circuit
    we die throughout life
Contained in our lives—
        like the canker at the apple's core? No
not like the canker but
the ripeness!
Or like mangoes, here in Solentiname, in summer
going slowly yellow, waiting
for the golden orioles . . .

                              the hors d'oeuvres
          in restaurants were never as good
          as in the advertisements
          nor the poem as good as we hoped
          nor the kiss.
          We have always desired more than we lacked
          We are Somozas seeking to own ever more haciendas
                    More More More
          nor yet just more, but something "different"
                The nuptials of desire
          The coition of perfect will is the act
          of dying.
                         We move among things with the air
          of having mislaid a most important
          briefcase.
                     Take escalators up and take them down.
          Enter the supermarket or the store,
          like anyone else, seeking the transcendental
          product.
                    We live as though waiting
          for an infinite assignation. Or
                                         to be called to the phone
          by the Ineffable.
          And are alone
          the grain that does not die, yet are alone.
          We sit at ease on deck and dream
                contemplating sea the colour of daiquiri
          waiting for someone to pass and smile at us and
          say hello.

          Not sleep but lucidity.
                Moving like sleepwalkers through the traffic
                         past the traffic-lights
          eye-open yet asleep
          savour a Manhatten as though asleep.

Not sleep but
lucidity is the true image of death
        of its illumination, of the blinding
splendour of death.
Nor is it the Kingdom of Forgetfulness. Memory
    is secretary to forgetfulness.
        She keeps the past in filing cabinets.
But when there is no more future merely an instant present
all that has been lived relives no longer as memories
and reality reveals itself entire
in one flash.

Poetry was a parting too
like death. Full of the
sadness of departing trains or planes
        the trains which pass in the night
        through the station of Brenes
        Cordobita below full of light
cante jondo in the depths of Granada...
In all beauty, a sadness
and a longing as in an alien land
    MAKE IT NEW
    ("a new heaven and a new earth")
but beyond this lucidity
the return to clichés, the return
to slogans.
It is only when we are not being practical
and concentrate on useless things that we
move out and find the world is opening out.
Dying is the act of being quite uninvolved
likewise : contemplation.
Love, love above all, as it were a foretaste
of death
    Kisses had the savour of death in them
        being

       involves being
           in some other being
  we only are when we love
But in this life we love only by fits and starts
and weakly
    We only love and are when we cease being
when we die
      a nakedness of being that we may make love
        make love not war
      going down to the love
      which is life

the city come from heaven which is not Atlantic City—
  nor the hereafter an *American way of life*
       Retirement in Florida
or one long limitless Weekend.
Death is a doorway opening
onto the universe
      No sign which says NO EXIT
and into ourselves
        (the journey
  into ourselves—
    not to Tokyo or Bangkok—
        that is the *appeal*
   "air hostess wearing a kimono,
Continental cuisine"
the real *appeal* of those Japanese Air Lines advertisements)
 A nuptial night, as Novalis put it
Not one of Boris Karloff's horror films
And natural, as is the fall of apples
subject to the law which draws the stars, or lovers
—There are no accidents
    just one more apple off the Tree
you're merely one more apple
Tom

                    We quit the body as one quits
                    a motel room
But you're not Wells's invisible man
            Nor like a ghost in a haunted house
                    We need no *mediums*.
And children knowing that there's really NO thing there
that we are immortal
Can napalm blot out life ?
                        Does the gas-chamber lead to nothingness?
    Are the Gospels just SF?
Jesus went into the room and put the mourners out
            That is why swans sing said Socrates
just before death
                    Come, Caddo, let us all ascend
                            to the great Village in the sky (*twice*)
—To which all buses and all aircraft go
            Not as to a destination
            but to the Infinite
            We fly towards life at the speed of light
As the foetus bursts the amniotic bag...
Or as cosmonauts...
                        —the coming forth
                        from the chrysalis
        A *happening*.
the climax
of one's life
                    dies natalis
            of this pre-natal life...
The womb of matter left at last behind
                        Not something absurd :
                        but a mystery
a doorway opening onto the universe
not onto the void
            (like the door into an elevator which is not there)
Definitive at last.

                    Such is the awakening of one man, one morning,
                         at the voice of a nurse in the hospital.
         And we no longer have but merely are
                         but merely are and are mere being
                                   The voice of the lover saying
                                      beloved take off your bra
The doorway opening
that no one can now close—
                         "God who bade us live"
much though we may hope to return
                    to the first linkage of atoms, to
                    unawareness.
                                   The bombs get bigger every day.
Necrophilia : flirting with death. The lust for what is dead
              (corpses, machines, money, trash)
and if they dream of a woman she is made
in the image of an automobile
         The irresistible attraction of the inorganic
                    Hitler was seen in World War I
                    crouched down to view a corpse
                    and would not move away
(the military, machines, or money, shit)
Gas-chambers by day and Wagner in the evening
"5 million" said Eichmann (or maybe 6)
Or else we wish to give death beauty treatment
The Loved Ones (do not call them dead)
made-up, manicured, and with a smile
in the Garden of Rest of the Whispering Glades
         cf THE AMERICAN WAY OF DEATH
    one or two martinis to forget his face
relax and watch TV
                         the joy of driving a Porsche
                            (*any line you choose*)
perhaps to wait for resurrection in deep-freeze

in liquid nitrogen at −197°
    (stored like the grain which never dies)
until the day when immortality comes cheap
After coffee, Benedictine
a sports-jacket to stay young, to keep death off
while waiting for the elixir of youth to be discovered
                the antidote
to dying.
Like the good cowboy in the films, who never dies.
        Seeking the Fountain of Youth in Miami,
the pleasures advertised in the Virgin Islands
Or sailing Lethe on board Onassis' yacht...

You did not seek to be a man who is a Name
whose face is recognized by all who read
the tabloid press
Your wilderness which flowered as the lily
was not Paradise Valley Hotel
        with cocktails served in the pool
beneath the palms
nor were your solitudes those of Lost Island
    with coconut-trees bending towards the sea
LOVE? *It's in the movies*
        the irruptions of eternity
        were brief—
Those of us who disbelieved this world's *Advertisements*
        dinner for two, "je t'adore"
                How to say love in Italian?
You said to me: the
        Gospel never mentions contemplation
No LSD
but the horror of God (or
        should we translate it "terror"?)
        His love like the radiation which touches not yet slays
and a void far greater than the Macrocosm!

        The only vision in your meditation
        that plane on the Miami to Chicago run
        and SAC's plane carrying the Bomb
           the days in which you wrote to me
My life is one of deepening contradiction and frequent darkness
Your *trip*? such a dull one
     a voyage into vast solitudes, expanse of nothingness
all chalklike
         black and white, *with no colour*
a watching the luminous ball, blue and rose like agate
Christmas on Broadway with songs and copulation
shining on the dusty waves of the Sea of Tranquillity
or the Sea of Crisis dead to the harsh horizon. And
like the glinting ball hung on a Christmas tree . . .

     Time? *IS money*
is *Time Magazine,* is a state of boredom, a nothing
    Time with a celebrity depicted on the cover

And that advertisement for Borden's Milk, under the rain
way back at Columbia, switching on
and switching off, only so fleetingly on
        kisses in a cinema
films and film-stars
all so fleeting
     GONE WITH THE WIND
although the dead stars may still smile in their beauty
on the screen
     the car breaks down, the fridge
is sent away to be repaired
        Her dress butter-yellow
          marmalade orange and strawberry pink
like a New Yorker ad imprinted on the memory
lipstick already smeared by kisses
farewells at the windows of planes bound
                for oblivion

shampoos for girls more distant than the Moon
or Venus
      Eyes more precious than the Stock Exchange
Nixon's inauguration long since past
the last image on the screen dissolved
and the streets of Washington swept clean
Time Alfonso Time? *Is money, mierda, shit*
time is but *The New York Times* and *Time*—
    And all things seemed to me like Coke . . .

        Proteins and nucleic acids
           ("how fair the numbers of their forms")
proteins and nucleic acids
          bodies are like gas to the touch
and beauty a bitter gas
like tear-gas
       Because the film of this world passes . . .
          like Coca-Cola
     or copulation *for*
     that matter
Cells are as ephemeral as flowers
          yet life is not
   protoplasm chromosomes yet
life is not
     "We live again" as the Comanches sang
    our lives are the rivers which
    flow down to life
now we see but as on television (darkly)
but later, face to face
       All perception but a trial of death
         beloved this is the pruning season
   The many kisses which you could not give will all be given
        the pomegranates are in bloom
all love but a *rehearsal* of death
    So we fear beauty

When Li Chi was carried off by the Duke of Chin
she wept until her tears had soaked her garments
but when once in the palace she regretted
having wept
The *San Juan de la* ✠ rounds the headland
some ducks
fly over
"the remote isles"
or "longing" as St John of the Cross called it
infinite longing
rend the garment of this sweet encounter
the Thracians mourned their births according to Herodotus
and sang their deaths—
It was in Advent, when the apple-trees down by the greenhouse
in Gethsemani are skeletal
and blossom white with frost
like frigidaires . . .
Alfonso in the madhouse said I don't believe it
when I told him that Pallais was dead
it must be politics he said
or something of that sort.
Do they still bury a camel with them
for the journey? and the whale-toothed clubs
with Fiji islanders?
Men's laughter at a joke proves they believe
in resurrection
or when a child wakes in the night and cries
and his mother soothes him
Evolution is towards more and more life
and it is irreversible
incompatible with the hypothesis
of the void
Yvy Mara ey
migrations sought it in the heartland of Brazil
("the land of no dying")

      Like mangoes here in summer in Solentiname
ripening
whilst there the whole novitiate is cowled in snow.

              The orioles
        seek out Deer Island where they sleep
you said to me
It is easy for us to approach him
We are strangers in the cosmos tourists really
                  having no dwelling here but just hotels
Like Yankee tourists
                everywhere
swift with the camera but never really knowing
          As one quits a motel room
             YANKEE GO HOME
Over Solentiname another evening dies
Tom
                  these sacred waters glitter
and then go slowly dull
time to light the Coleman
      all joy is union
    absence of others, pain :
               Western Union
The cable from the Abbot of Gethsemani was yellow
     WE REGRET TO INFORM YOU etc . . .
and I just said
okay
              Where the dead unite and
                  are with the cosmos
                        one
     "which is far better" (Phil. 1.23)
Just as the moon dies and is reborn . . .
        death is union and
           one is at last oneself
               in union with the world

because death thus is better
the flame-trees bloom tonight, scattering life
      (their renunciation is a scarlet flower)
death is union
         half-moon over Solentiname
      with three men
one does not die alone
      (the Great Lodge of Reunion) the Ojibway
and the world is even deeper
Where Algonquin spirits wearing spirit moccasins
hunt beaver spirits over spirit snow
         we thought the moon was so far off
dying is not to leave the world
but to dive into it
to reach the "alternative" universe
      the *underground*
out of this world's *Establishment*, out of space-time
neither Johnson nor yet Nixon
   there are no tigers there
         say the Malays
(an Isle in the West)
      which go down to the sea
      which is life
Where the dead are met together oh Netzahualcóyotl
or "Heart of the World"
      Hemingway, Raissa, Barth, Alfonso Cortés
the world is even deeper
      Hades, to which Christ descended
         centre : belly (Matt. 12.40)
      SIGN OF JONAS
      the depths of all visible beauty
where the great cosmic whale swims on
replete with prophets
      The kisses which you did not give will all be given
Is transformed.

... "as one lay buried in one's mother's womb ..."
                    a Cuna headman said to Keeler
Life does not end but is transformed
       another wombed existence say the Koguis
who therefore place their dead in hammocks
in the foetal pose—
        Plato said it was an old belief
that there are people in Hades
            who had come from here ...
Beziers, the cathedral as one sees it from the train
       Nothing one recalls with yearning is lost
            the scent of the Midi
the red tower of Saint Jacques down by the Tarn
lights white and green, in Paris : on the Eiffel
           Tower : *C-I-T-R-O-E-N*
Lax travelled with circuses
           and knows what it is
to take the Big Top down by lamplight
leave the site bare
and travel in a lorry through the night to another city
And when the wife of Chuang Tzu died
Chuang Tzu did not mourn
     Hui Tzu found him singing and dancing and
using the rice-pan as a drum
       the hammock is the placenta, the hammock's
rope the umbilical cord
     "your headaches will do you no harm"
        seed—plant—seed
     the dialectics of destruction
          I speak
of wheat. Living
is for dying, for giving in the scattering of life
Until the masked and white-gloved coming
of the secret agent
        whose identifying letters are unknown to us

To give ourselves to death with love
And
if the stars die not
each stays alone
if they do not go back to cosmic dust
    seed—plant—seed
death is union
     not in Junction City
Or, as the Cunas likewise say,
   "One day we would like a good dinner"
We clamour for the total giving of the Lover
Or as the Abbot Hesychius said :
Frequent meditation upon death is
"as when fish disport themselves in a quiet sea
and dolphins jump rejoicing"
   And, just as the moon dies . . .
    They are on an island, Columbus
  was told in Haiti, together on an island
  eating mameias in the night—
Or, again, the isle *Boluto*, East of Tonga
a place of joy and flowers and spiritual bread-fruit
"apparently electrocuted"
     Laughlin wrote me
"at least it was over quickly"
     the tearing of the veil
between the soul and God . . . And :
. . . since love desires the passage should be brief . . .
  the soul's rivers of love
  flow thither to join the sea
arriving lovely as Joan Baez in a big black car
You used to laugh at ads in the New Yorker
  yet here's one by Pan Am
  **Ticket to Japan
    To Bangkok
     To Singapore

>*All the way to the mysteries***

A ticket for contemplation? Yes
>A ticket for contemplation.
>>Also for death

>*All the way to the mysteries*

Advertisements are manuals
of meditation, says Corita
>>Sister Corita

and advertising something more. Don't take them
at face value.
Biological death : it must be politics
or something of that sort.
>General Electric, fate
>>a jet from Vietnam to bear the corpse

but once this winter is over, at Eastertide
or Whitsun
you'll hear the Trappist tractors near your cemetery
Trappist yet noisy, fresh furrowing the earth
So as to plant, new Mayas, ancient maize.
—The time of resurrection for the locusts
>and the Caterpillars

Like the banana-tree which dies to produce fruit, Hawäians say.
>You were empty
>>with all love given, you

had nothing left to give
>>Ready to go to Bangkok

To start the beginning of the new
accept the dying of the old
>>Our lives
>>flowing down to life

on taking off from California
>the windows of the jet wept tears

>of joy!

At last you've reached Solentiname (it wasn't *practical*)

after the Dalai Lama, and Himalayan buses
painted like dragons
                "the remote isles"; you're here
with your silent Tzus and Fus
Kung Tzu, Lao Tzu, Meng Tzu, Tu Fu—and Nicanor Parra—
and in all places; as easy to communicate with you
as it is with God (or just as difficult)
      like the whole cosmos in one drop of dew
this morning on the path to the latrine
Elias taken skyward in a chariot of cosmic energy
        or the Papuan tribe that seeing the telegraph
        made a small model
        to talk with the dead
Valerius Maximus tells us that the Celts
lent money to be repaid beyond the grave.

             All the kisses given or not given.
That is why swans sing said Socrates
the fan still whirling
at your heart
          We only love and only are on dying
    The final deed the gift of all one's being
okay

Glossary

Ahau Mayan sun god, after whom the last day of the 20-day month was named. The 260 days of the "sacred" year (not the 365-day "civil" year) were designated by numbers from 1 to 13 followed by one of twenty day-names: e.g., 11 Ahau. For *Katun 11 Ahau*, see *katun*.

ayllu One of the communal landholdings into which the Inca territory was divided; also the community which cultivated it. The entire Inca world-picture was based on this "collective" concept.

cante jondo Flamenco singing.

chicha Fermented drink, made from maize throughout the old Inca territories.

chilan Mayan soothsayer, prophet and oracle – member of a particular class of priests specializing in divination.

Cihuacóatl Aztec goddess known as "The Serpent Lady", or earth mother, representing the feminine principle of the universe.

corrido Mexican popular song in ballad form.

huehuetl Aztec wooden drum beaten with the fingers, emitting two distinct tones.

katun Mayan period of 7200 days (just under 20 years), named after the day it ended. Each name recurred roughly every 256 years, and the Spaniards arrived in the first year of one particular Katun 11 Ahau (i.e., 1541). Since each cycle is re-enacted, "Katun 11 Ahau" denotes a recurring period of disaster.

latifundio Very large *hacienda* (agricultural estate) owned by a *latifundista* – usually an absentee landlord – and run on semi-feudal lines.

macehual (pl. *macehuales*; Nahuatl *maceualli*) Member of the peasant class in Aztec society.

milpa Mayan field, more specifically a plot of maize. Ancient Mayan "cities" were not "cities" in our sense, but ceremonial centres sustained by large populations who lived in villages among the *milpas*.

Netzahualcóyotl (1402–1472) King of Texcoco, near Tenochtitlán, and the finest named Nahuatl poet.

nopal Mexican name for prickly pear.

puna Sparse grazing land in the Andes, usually above 12,000 feet.

quena Andean flute, generally made of cane but sometimes of bone.

Quetzalcóatl Aztec god known as "The Plumed Serpent", responsible in his aspect as the Morning Star for the daily resurrection of the sun.

Tahuantinsuyu (lit. land of "The Four Horizons") The Inca empire.

Tenochtitlán Aztec capital, where the central zone of Mexico City stands today.

teponaztli Aztec musical instrument. A wooden cylinder with an I-shaped incision whose tongues produced two different notes when struck with rubber-tipped mallets.

Tláloc Aztec rain god known as "Lord of all Sources of Water" – a very ancient fertility deity.

yaraví (pl. *yaravíes*) The best-known Andean folk-song form, the melancholy quality of whose music is reinforced by the text.